Flora Whitney Miller
1897–1986

1942–1966	President, Whitney Museum of American Art
1966–1974	Chairman
1974–1986	Honorary Chairman

Flora Whitney Miller

Her Life, Her World

Whitney Museum of American Art

Library of Congress
Cataloging-in-
Publication Data

Flora Whitney Miller :
her life, her world.

   1. Miller, Flora
Whitney.   2. Art pa-
trons—United States—
Biography.   3. Whitney
family.   4. Whitney
Museum of American
Art.   I. Whitney Mu-
seum of American Art.
N5220.M578F56
1987   709'.2'4
[B]   87-6158
ISBN 0-87427-054-5

Copyright © 1987
Whitney Museum of American Art
945 Madison Avenue
New York, N.Y. 10021

This memorial tribute
was published for the
membership of the
Whitney Museum of
American Art and the
family and friends of
Flora Whitney Miller.
It was presented at a re-
ception at the Whitney
Museum on Thursday,
April 30, 1987.

Frontispiece: The world in which my mother grew up
is captured in this portrait by Howard Cushing,
which he painted in his Newport studio, c. 1908. Its
captivating beauty and the sensuousness of the
fabrics, flowers, and wall painting emphasize the
languorous, dreamy quality then associated with
becoming a young lady in this special, hermetic
world. I feel the painting represents the prelude to a
journey that led Flora to become the vibrant, mature
woman we remember, a woman who guided a great
institution to *its* maturity.

                    Flora Miller Biddle

The death of Flora Whitney Miller, daughter of the founder of the Whitney Museum of American Art, in July 1986, represents the loss of the most direct and forceful association between the Whitney Museum of American Art and its origins.

As the child of two of the greatest families in the United States, the Whitneys and the Vanderbilts, Flora grew up in an environment of immense wealth and power, dominated by men who built American industry and transportation. She embraced the challenge of her legacy with as much determination as her forebears, and achieved her own position of strength in a world very far removed from that of her youth—a postwar world in which the power and fortunes of families such as her own were diminished by the distribution of wealth. It was she who realized that if the Whitney Museum were to thrive in the future, it would have to develop from a private, family-run museum to a public institution. Flora guided the Museum through this critical period in its history. We feel that the story of Flora's life makes her accomplishments as the leader of a twentieth-century institution all the more remarkable and hope that as you read this memoir you will share our respect and love for her.

T.A.

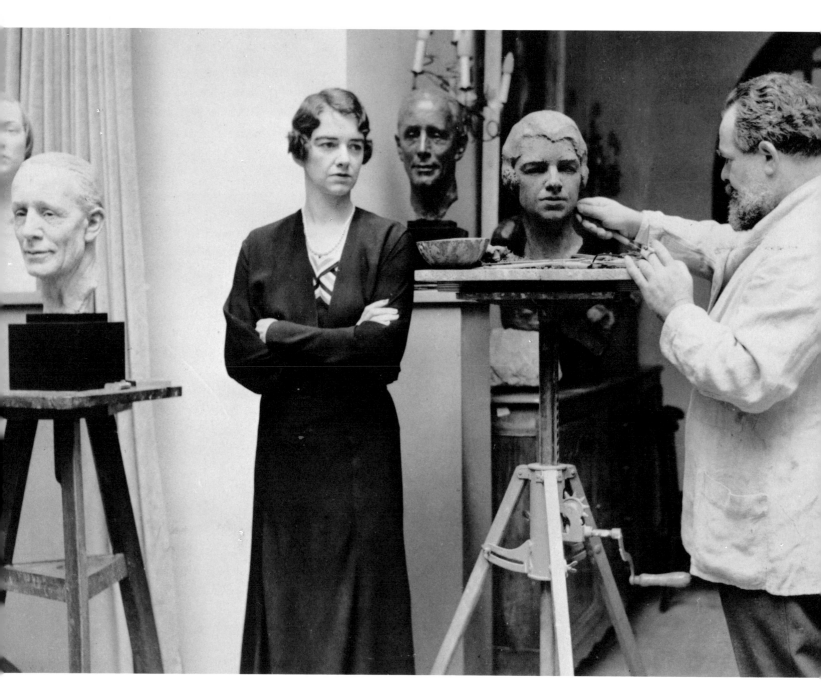

Flora posing for Jo Davidson as he works on her
portrait, 1933.

Family and Friends Who Remember
Flora Whitney Miller
in the Album of Reminiscences and Photographs

Tom Armstrong

Ivor G. Balding

John I.H. Baur

Flora Miller Biddle

Bronson Winthrop Chanler

Eliza Parkinson Cobb

Gertrude Conner

Frederick A. Cushing

C. Douglas Dillon

Brendan Gill

Lloyd Goodrich

Michael Graves

Margaret Mellon Hitchcock

Fiona Irving

Philip Johnson

Seymour H. Knox

Nancy Perkins Lancaster

John LeBoutillier

Pamela T. LeBoutillier

Howard Lipman

John L. Marion

William A. Marsteller

James A. Michener

Devereux Milburn, Jr.

Leverett S. Miller

Roy R. Neuberger

Jacqueline Kennedy Onassis

Sandra Payson

William P.T. Preston

S. Dillon Ripley

Blanchette H. Rockefeller

Benno C. Schmidt

Linda Shearer

David M. Solinger

Beatrice Straight

Whitney Tower

Gloria Vanderbilt

Frederick H. von Stade

Diana Vreeland

Betsey Whitney

Cornelius Vanderbilt Whitney

Contents

Introduction

Flora Miller Biddle

Time spent with our parents was precious. Their lives seemed like the flaming plum puddings carried in at Christmas lunch, and we longed to be grown up so we could be part of the magic. In the meantime, their enthusiasm and their love nourished us four children.

Our mother was the center, the one we all wanted there, and countless memories of her have flooded back since she died. She read to us—Kipling's jungle tales of Mowgli or "The White Seal" to me, feverish in bed, firelight flickering. "Gamoo" (my grandmother) had read them to *her*, she said, and she relished the stories along with the memory of her beloved mother. I in turn read to my mother. The acrid smell of gunpowder still surrounds me in recollections of reading to her in a cornstalk blind on a dove shoot in the winter fields of South Carolina. On present-day fishing trips with my own family, I always envision Mum casting her dry fly gracefully into a still pool, thrilled at the trout's rise and the beauty of the Adirondack stream, infusing us all with a lifelong addiction to mountains, lakes, and fishing.

She made every birthday a scintillating cascade of fun and an affirmation of our young selves. Christmas was an exciting, glittering time of sharing. On New Year's Eve we gazed enchanted at our parents' witty, elegant fancy-dress costumes, at the gaiety and glamour of their friends, and at the romance of their dances.

She flowed into a room, elegant, smelling delicious, with hugs and kisses and a surprised look. She seemed to expect that something delightful would happen, and indeed it

Facing page: Flora Whitney Miller and her daughter Flora, c. 1950, seated in the living room of Flora Miller's residence at 10 Gracie Square beneath the 1941 portrait of Gertrude Vanderbilt Whitney by Eugene Speicher. Speicher was the most accomplished and respected portrait painter of his time. He had first exhibited at the Whitney Museum of American Art in 1933, having initially shown at the Whitney Studio Club in 1917. Through funds provided by Gertrude Vanderbilt Whitney, the Museum had purchased nine paintings and five drawings by Speicher by the time of her death in 1942.

Right: Flora reading to her daughter Flora in Aiken, c. 1933.

often did. Everyone's best adventures, most of all those of the heart, were saved for her, especially when her grandchildren came to call; she had a marvelous rapport with the young.

At some point in our young lives, she made us aware of family tradition. Our grandmother and the Whitney Museum of American Art came to symbolize the creative and enduring aspects of our heritage, and all that was exotic and mysterious in our mother's life away from us, when she visited the magical city of New York. Realization grew that this grandmother was a remarkable woman—pioneer, artist, patron, personality. How natural to admire and adore this heroine, to absorb Mum's profound conviction that the Museum her mother had founded was vitally important for our country and was our responsibility to care for. After Gertrude Vanderbilt Whitney's death in 1942, Mum became the leader of the Museum for over twenty-five years, thus ensuring its survival, independence, continuity, and growth. With grace and passion, she communicated to me her love for art, for artists, and for the Whitney Museum of American Art, always hoping that her descendants would see to its future.

This love is one of her greatest gifts to me, one that has brought countless rewards and joys, including the special closeness of working together, and the deep consciousness of three generations of women in a family brought together through the Museum we have loved so deeply in our different ways.

The extraordinary concern and understanding of Joan Clark, a Trustee of the Whitney Museum of American Art, Phyllis Wattis, a member of the Museum's National Committee, and family and friends who remembered my mother at the time of her death, have made possible this tribute to my mother, Flora Whitney Miller, and I am profoundly grateful. To realize dreams is one aspect of Joan Clark's generous, creative nature, and it was her special gift that encouraged this project and helped realize Tom Armstrong's vision of a beloved person, expressed in a photographic essay that shows the full range of my mother's life and reveals the leadership and continuity she gave to the Whitney Museum during her adult years. My profound thanks to Tom for this enduring memorial. B.H. Friedman, biographer of my grandmother, Gertrude Vanderbilt Whitney, has eloquently placed my mother within her time and her family. I salute and bless him for his care and sensitivity. Many have contributed their special thoughts and feelings to this book, and the words of others have been taken from older letters or diaries. To each and every one who has thus given, my family's and my lasting appreciation.

Facing page: Four generations of Flora's family (from left): her mother, Gertrude Vanderbilt Whitney; her grandmother, Alice Gwynne (Mrs. Cornelius) Vanderbilt; Flora; and her first child, Pamela Tower.

Flora Miller Biddle, daughter of Flora and G. Macculloch Miller, became a Trustee of the Whitney Museum of American Art in 1958 and has served as Vice President (1962–77), President (1977–85), and is now Chairman of the Board.

Flora Whitney Miller

A Brief Biography and Personal Reminiscence

B.H. Friedman

Flora Payne Whitney, the eldest child of Gertrude Vanderbilt and Harry Payne Whitney, was born July 29, 1897 and died this past summer, eleven days before her eighty-ninth birthday.

Throughout her childhood, her years at the Brearley School, and her coming out, her name was frequently in the newspapers and magazines, as were those of her younger brother and sister, Cornelius Vanderbilt (Sonny) Whitney and Barbara Whitney.

As with other members of the Four Hundred, Gertrude and Harry Whitney and their children were news. The Vanderbilt-Whitney wedding joined two of the most prominent and powerful families in the United States. Gertrude's father was Cornelius Vanderbilt II, president of the New York Central Railroad. Harry's was William C. Whitney, lawyer, businessman, brother-in-law of Standard Oil's Oliver Payne, and Secretary of the Navy under Grover Cleveland. The parties in the Whitney's Fifth Avenue mansion, in their home on some seven hundred acres in Old Westbury, Long Island, and in their other residences in Newport, the Adirondacks, Aiken, Saratoga, and various shooting boxes in Georgia, Tennessee, and Yorkshire were all news. And so were their activities as amateurs (in the root sense) of sports and the arts.

Flora Whitney's generation was virtually the last in which members of "society" were the heroes and heroines of American fantasy. Entrenched wealth—the often overlapping categories of business leaders and inventors, as well as the professionals who served them (lawyers, doctors, architects, clergymen)—appeared in publications as frequently as the great personalities of theater and opera, of literature and the arts. The professional athletes and movie stars (Babe Ruth, Jack Dempsey, Mary Pickford, etc.) who would eventually drive society off the front page and the magazine cover, were born just a few years before Flora Whitney, as were the filmmakers and the writers of the stories, plays, and songs that would commemorate the magic and style of her generation—Scott Fitzgerald, John P. Marquand, Philip Barry and, perhaps most of all, Cole Porter, who wrote retrospectively during the Depression:

> You're the top!
> You're the tower of Babel
> You're the top!
> You're the Whitney stable

and

> When folks who still can ride in jitneys
> Find out Vanderbilts and Whitneys
> Lack baby clo'es
> Anything goes.

Until formal schooling, Flora spent most of her time with governesses while her parents traveled. At the age of six or seven she understood her father's passion for riding, horse racing, polo, hunting and shooting. All of this she witnessed in Old Westbury. Every season there were new horses and ponies, more trophies and loving cups. Frequently she heard of her father's successful bids for thoroughbreds and of their victories in important races. By 1909, she was following his entry into British racing and the next year his "invasion" of British polo. As captain of the Meadow Brook Club's "Big Four," he was determined to bring back the America Challenge Cup, in England since 1886. The Big Four won. Flora and her family were received by the King and Queen and by other members of the British aristocracy, including her cousin Consuelo Vanderbilt, the former Duchess of Marlborough; her aunt and uncle, Pauline Whitney and Almeric Paget; and the Hurlingham team's Lord Wodehouse.

Thus far, her mother's real interests—in sculpture and in encouraging American art by buying and commissioning it—were relatively private. As a child Flora visited Gertrude's studio at Bryant Park and, later, studios at 19 MacDougal Alley in Greenwich Village, on the grounds in Old Westbury, on Cliff Walk in Newport, and in Paris. Flora watched her

Facing page, left: Flora at the age when she appeared in the newspapers as "Cornelius Vanderbilt's Baby Sweetheart."

Facing page, right: Illustration of Flora Payne Whitney, c. 1900, from an unidentified New York City newspaper.

Right: Gertrude Vanderbilt and Harry Payne Whitney with their infant daughter, Flora Payne Whitney, in their home at 2 West Fifty-seventh Street, 1897.

Throughout her life, Flora kept carefully annotated albums of family photographs and newspaper clippings. This followed a family tradition of three generations, and they are the source for the photograph album pages in this book. Most of the handwritten notations were made by Flora.
Following page: Album page with photographs of Flora and her fiancé, Quentin Roosevelt, at the Roosevelt home, Sagamore Hill, before his departure for Europe as a member of the Air Arm of the U.S. Army in World War I, c. 1917.

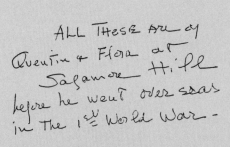

ALL THESE ARE OF
Quentin & Flora at
Sagamore Hill
before he went overseas
in the 1st World War —

Quentin & F.P.W.

Quentin & F.P.W.

On August 4, 1916, Flora made her debut in Newport at a supper dance in the newly built Whitney ballroom. The list of almost five hundred guests, running two columns in the *Times*, "brought together the entire Summer Colony." Gertrude in black with jet trim and Flora in white with silver trim, both tall and slim, complemented each other as they received guests against a contrastingly colorful background of flowers. Later, as Flora danced with her dinner partner Quentin Roosevelt—a stocky, solid young man, a "Teddy Bear" like his father—everyone remarked on the attractiveness of the couple. The war in Europe still seemed far away.

That moment didn't last. Flora and Quentin had hardly become engaged, when the United States entered the war and he enlisted in what was then called the Air Arm of the U.S. Army. For almost two years Flora and Quentin corresponded while she learned typing and shorthand and worked on projects to help the war effort and, with her mother, on other projects at what had become the Whitney Studio Club. On July 14, 1918, Quentin was shot down and killed inside the German lines. Before making a public announcement, Theodore Roosevelt broke the news to Flora. In a small sculpture by her mother for which Flora posed soon after, she is gaunt, her head bowed, her eyes sunken.

mother's ambitions grow from intimate sketches in clay and plaster to commissions, involving teams of artisans, for such monuments as the Aztec Fountain and the Titanic Memorial, both in Washington, D.C. During the same years, she saw contemporary American paintings and sculpture flowing steadily into Gertrude's studios and homes—work very different from the established foreign masterpieces collected by her parents' relatives and friends. As early as 1908, Gertrude Whitney bought four of the seven paintings sold at the Macbeth Gallery's exhibition of The Eight, and she continued to support these artists and many more of the period. She also commissioned murals and portraits by Robert Henri, Jo Davidson, and Guy Pène du Bois, among others. In short, from her earliest years on, Flora saw contemporary art, met contemporary artists, and identified with her mother's commitment to both.

Top of page: "Miss Flora Whitney," *Vogue,* September 15, 1916: "Miss Whitney, the daughter of Mr. Harry Payne Whitney, is one of the first as well as one of the foremost of the débutantes of the new season. She was introduced to society at Newport early in August, and her début dance was held in the huge blue and yellow ballroom which has just been added to the Whitneys' Newport house. Miss Whitney is the first débutante in the Vanderbilt and Whitney families since Countess Széchényi, who was Miss Gladys Vanderbilt, and Mrs. Willard Straight, who was Miss Dorothy Whitney, made their respective débuts."

Right: Gertrude Vanderbilt Whitney, *Flora,* 1919, bronze, collection of Abby and B.H. Friedman.

During the following months of depression, Flora worked as Theodore Roosevelt's secretary; then, after his death in January 1919, for the Navy Department; and then for the Women's Republican National Executive Committee, in Washington, where she lived with Quentin's sister Alice Roosevelt Longworth. Finally, by spring, she felt able to make a trip to Paris and went with her Aunt Dorothy who, having lost her husband Willard Straight at the end of the war, was also in need of cheering up. Dorothy, Harry Whitney's youngest sister, only ten years older than Flora, proved to be a perfect companion. They stayed at the Ritz; visited the sculptors Jo Davidson and Herbert Haseltine, who had sculpted the Big Four; and were soon shopping for themselves and for Gertrude at such fashionable couturiers as Poiret and Chanel. By the end of summer, Flora was in much higher spirits. She was wearing clothes that at first she thought were "too awful"—dresses "shorter and shorter," evening gowns with "nothing to them at all, literally nothing above the waist in the back,

Flora in the office of the Republican Women's Headquarters in Washington, D.C., where she worked as volunteer secretary to the Chairman of its National Executive Committee, Mrs. Medill McCormick, while staying with Alice Roosevelt Longworth, Quentin Roosevelt's sister, in 1919.

and cut entirely out under the arms." Her hair was bobbed. She smoked (in private, anyway). She was a prototypical "flapper."

Next year, while studying short-story writing at Columbia University and doing some sculpting at home, Flora became engaged to Roderick Tower who, like Quentin Roosevelt, had been in the air corps and was a ruggedly handsome complement to Flora's delicate beauty. Roderick—the son of Charlemagne Tower of Philadelphia, former United States ambassador to Russia and to Germany—had graduated from Harvard in 1915 and had subsequently spent much of his time in New York City, where he had a seat on the Stock Exchange. Their wedding, April 19, 1920 at St. Bartholomew's, attracted a huge crowd, watching the steady procession of limousines filled with Vanderbilts, Whitneys, Sloanes, Webbs, Twomblys, Shepards, Pagets, Barneys, Harrimans, Morgans, Belmonts, Pulitzers— the names, the faces, once again recognizable from newspapers and magazines.

After a honeymoon trip to Honolulu and Japan, Flora and Rod settled initially in Los Angeles, which he used as a base for oil exploration throughout the West and later in Mexico. In Flora's diary, there are many indications of her loneliness and nostalgia: commemorations of Theodore Roosevelt's birth and of Quentin's (who would have been twenty-three in 1920); resentment of Rod's constant business trips, some as long as a month, and of his time on the "graveyard shift, 10:30 p.m. to 6:30 a.m. Horrible. I sleep all night and he sleeps all day." Blank stretches of silence are relieved partially by lists of books read, movies seen, cultural events attended and, finally, by the birth of Pamela Tower in 1921 and Whitney Tower two years later. One feels Flora's excitement as baby pictures appear on the pages and as weights and first steps are recorded. There seems to be a change in mood, a determination to make the marriage work. Flora studies geology, visits various oil fields. . . . Rod reads Lytton Strachey's *Queen Victoria* aloud

Top:
The wedding party of the marriage of Flora Whitney and Roderick Tower, April 19, 1920, at St. Bartholomew's Church, New York City. Front row (from left): Cornelia, Alice, and Gladys Széchényi; Beatrice and Whitney Straight. Back row (from left): Geoffrey Tower, Flora, Roderick, and Flora's sister Barbara.

Bottom:
Flora and G. Macculloch Miller on camelback in front of the Great Pyramid and Sphinx in Egypt during their honeymoon; they had been married in Cairo on February 24, 1927.

Flora, her husband, G. Macculloch Miller, her daughter Pamela, and Kay Sage, c. 1935. Kay Sage, Flora's classmate at Foxcroft and close friend, was an accomplished Surrealist painter, married at one time to Yves Tanguy.

to her. . . . They try. . . . And then, the day after their fourth anniversary, they "dined alone in [her] room & talked & talked—dreadful—& decided it definitely—what hurts! what hurts—." Flora got her divorce quietly in La Bourbole, France, then joined her mother in Paris and made several sculptures there. Two were included in the Whitney Studio Club's tenth annual exhibition, one appropriately titled *Crisis*.

Flora and her children moved into a new house on the Old Westbury property, originally designed by the architect William Adams Delano for her and Rod. There, and in the other Whitney homes, and on trips abroad, she saw a great deal of such old friends as Vincent Astor, Ralph Pulitzer, the book publisher "Tim" Coward, and, finally, most frequently, G. Macculloch Miller. "Cully," a future architect, shared her interests in the arts and in society. He had talent as a draftsman and made sure, quick sketches and paintings of family, friends, and settings, often accompanied by light commemorative verse. (*Jingles by Cully*, a collection of his sometimes "naughty" illustrated poems, was published posthumously.)

When Flora and Cully became engaged, Gertrude invited them and Flora's children to join her at the end of a trip to the Middle East. Their marriage, February 24, 1927 in Cairo, at which Cully placed an elephant-hair ring on Flora's finger, was witnessed by Jo and Yvonne Davidson. The next year Flora gave birth to Flora Macculloch Miller, and in 1931 Leverett Saltonstall Miller was born.

Harry Whitney died in 1930, just after Gertrude had announced her intention to expand the social and exhibition programs and the physical facilities of the Whitney Galleries (which had grown out of the Whitney Studio and the Whitney Studio Club) into a museum with a permanent collection based on the five hundred or so American works purchased by her since early in the century. This long-term dream was encouraged by Harry during his lifetime and now by Flora, who participated in some of the planning. Cully's firm, Noel and Miller, served as architects for the new building, which integrated four houses at 8-14 West Eighth Street, adjoining Gertrude's studio on MacDougal Alley.

The Whitney Museum of American Art opened on November 16, 1931 with a daylong celebration. The institution was praised by President Herbert Hoover and Governor Alfred E. Smith, and it was attacked in some journals for exhibiting such "incomprehensible" works as Stuart Davis' *Egg Beater No. 1*, Charles Demuth's *My Egypt*, Max Weber's *Chinese Restaurant*, and Georgia O'Keeffe's *Skunk Cabbage*. By 1931 standards, the opening was enormous. About 5,000 invited guests crowded the small museum—artists, some established, some still students; Village bohemians; dealers; architects; writers; museum directors and curators; art patrons. By seven that evening, Gertrude, Flora, some family members and close friends, and a few favorite artists—Stuart Davis, John Sloan, and Eugene Speicher—had retreated to the apartment of Juliana Force, the Museum's director. There the party continued, and there began a tradition—an *ambition* for some artists—which would last until Mrs. Force's death in 1948: to be invited to The Apartment after an opening.

From 1931 on, Flora was in The Apartment often, sometimes representing her mother at openings Gertrude was unable to attend. In the early thirties she and Cully and the four children began spending more time in Aiken, South Carolina, where Flora was one of the founders of the Aiken Day School and was active on its board. In 1936, she became a Trustee of the Whitney Museum as well, and six years later, after her mother's death, she became its President. During these years, Flora and Cully traveled frequently—to Europe through 1935; after that, as the political climate became more ominous, to the Caribbean, South America, and Canada.

Peggy Bacon, *The Social Graces*, 1935, drypoint, collection of the Whitney Museum of American Art. Illustrated is one of the frequent parties in the apartment of Juliana Force, first Director of the Whitney Museum, above the Whitney Museum on Eighth Street. Mrs. Force is shown dancing with her partner in the upper right.

However, from 1942 until 1961 she supported the Museum almost single-handedly and, in 1954, saw it through its first move, from Eighth Street to larger quarters on Fifty-fourth. There, it quickly outgrew its space and was also dominated by the Museum of Modern Art. She began thinking of a second move to a still larger building with a more separate identity. For this she wanted, indeed needed, outside help and, for the first time, invited a non-family group to join the Museum's board. As one of this group of seven, all active in the recently formed Friends of the Whitney Museum, I first met Flora Miller.

Even in her early sixties, Flora was still an unusually attractive woman, still something of a flapper. Though her hair was graying, she wore it short as she had since the twenties, and she had remained slim, suggesting the stemlike elegance of a flower. She stooped slightly but somehow this accentuated the attentiveness of her bright hazel eyes and small up-turned nose. She dressed more quietly than her mother but just as distinctively—in Chanel and Balenciaga suits and often in pants, long before they became fashionable. Her voice was as carefully modulated as her clothes. She punctuated her conversation with vowel sounds, particularly the exclamation *oh!* and the adverbs *too* and *so*.

During the planning of the Museum's present building at Seventy-fifth and Madison, I saw Flora Miller frequently and got to know her family, particularly her daughter Flora Irving, an active member of the board, along with her husband Michael, Marcel Breuer's associate architect on the new project. We had meetings occasionally at the Miller's apartment at 10 Gracie Square and in their Old Westbury home, both filled with memorabilia. In addition to art collected by Gertrude and sculpture made by her, there were many works in both places that reflected Flora's sometimes more eccentric taste—paintings by her close friend Kay Sage and by such better known Surrealists and Magic Realists as Peter Blume, Paul Cadmus, Loren MacIver, and George Tooker, as well as many works by Charles Burchfield, one of her favorite artists; watercolors by Cully; fanciful bedroom furniture in Old Westbury designed by Max Kuehne, stylized Art Deco pieces in New York contrasting with a "Venetian Baroque" piano.

When the present Museum opened in 1966, Flora Miller was elected Chairman of the Board, and David Solinger, a founder of the Friends, was elected President. At about the same time, John I. H. Baur succeeded Lloyd Goodrich as Director. Throughout these changes, complicated by pride and politics, Flora Miller was the queenly constant, the one person to whom everyone turned for approval. She, more than anyone else, represented the Museum and understood her mother's dream, a dream delicately balanced between democratic enthusiasm and professional caution. I never heard an unkind word spoken by or about Flora Miller. Shy and unaggressive, she symbolized a sort of privileged assurance that was above political ambition.

In the early seventies, soon after Cully's death and after the publication of my biography of Jackson Pollock, the two Floras approached me regarding a biography of Gertrude Vanderbilt Whitney. My first thought was of a short elegant book, something like Calvin Tomkins' *Living Well Is the Best Revenge*. Ultimately, Flora Irving and I collaborated on a detailed chronicle edited down to just under seven hundred printed pages. During the nearly five years we worked on this project, inevitably I got to know Flora Miller better and came to understand the extent to which she had subordinated much of her life to her mother's. She had saved everything of Gertrude's and now opened it all to us—family homes, attics and closets, journals and albums, bundles of letters. When we were through, Flora Irving showed her the original draft of the book and read some of it to her aloud. Afterwards, Flora Miller wrote me a letter in which I can hear her voice even now:

Dear Bob,

Really you are terrific! The book truly is the very best—and the new title "Lives of [not ultimately used by Doubleday] G.V.W." is so appealing and will make everyone, including all those Cayce followers [the spiritualist "Sleeping Prophet" Edgar Cayce] want to read it. The cheerful [scenes] and those that are "painfully intimate" make her whole life come *Alive*.

I read the last part in the early afternoon as I was sure if I waited until evening it would be so on my mind that it would be hard to go to sleep. There are things that one never forgets about someone you love, and you brought back many to me—and also things that I never knew—and one man I never heard of—and now I can't remember his name.

It is wonderful, Bob, and I just hope I'm alive when it comes out.

My love—and to Abby too.

Flora

I replied:

Dear Flora,

I was so pleased to receive your letter. But you deserve credit for much that is good about the book. It simply could not have been done without your love for your mother, your commitment to the meaning of her life, and your preservation of her memorabilia. Beyond all that, I greatly appreciate the confidence you have shown in me and, of course, in Flora.

As to your being alive when the book comes out, please stay with us. It is an odd accident that from working on this biography I know details of your life that I don't know concerning members of my own family. I wish I had known your mother. Knowing her, through documents and photographs and her own work, has been very rewarding but still not as much so as knowing you in person. I told Flora when I began working with her on this project that you mean to me what the Princesse de Guermantes meant to Proust. By that I meant that you represent for me a sort of aristocratic ideal, a grace and nobility of spirit. I feel that even more strongly now and always will.

Love, Bob

In 1977, the year of these letters, Flora Irving (soon to become Flora Biddle), was elected President of the Museum; David Solinger, Chairman; Flora Miller, Honorary Chairman. Three years earlier, Jack Baur had retired and Tom Armstrong became Director. Again, during these changes—simple in summary, complicated in life—Flora Miller's influence was steady, calming and, in every sense, charming. She was very proud of her daughter's taking over the leadership of the Museum, and from then on, largely because of failing health, she herself played a less active role in policy decisions. She came only occasionally to Museum meetings and other functions, most often to welcome new members of the enlarging Board of Trustees. However, as plans developed to expand the Museum once again, she sold her most valuable painting, J.M.W. Turner's *Juliet and Her Nurse*, inherited from her mother through Harry's uncle, Oliver Payne, and contributed part of the proceeds to the building fund. Typically, she was embarrassed by the publicity surrounding this sale, which established a then record price of $6.4 million.

Flora with her "fishing rod" cane seated with Robert W. Wilson, Trustee of the Whitney Museum of American Art since 1978, and John Ellis, her daughter Flora's assistant at the Whitney Museum, at the party she hosted in Gertrude Vanderbilt Whitney's studio in Old Westbury for members of the new National Committee of the Whitney Museum of American Art during the weekend of their first meeting, May 18, 1980.

During her last years, we exchanged letters on our birthdays, which were two days apart. Each year her letter became sadder—never self-pitying but increasingly full of intimations of mortality. When Flora was eighty, she wrote, "One of the things age produces is forgetfulness—I think I mind more than most people because I had such a good memory." And her letters were full, too, of phrases like "I just nearly die of it," phrases she used of ordinary things (in this case a novel she was reading) but surrounded now, for me anyway, by darkening clouds.

We continued to see each other occasionally. I remember a beautiful spring afternoon at the Belmont track, rooting for a horse owned by Lev Miller and talking about various articles on thoroughbred racing written by her other son Whitty Tower. I remember her also at Old Westbury, reading

the *Times* (for which she always wore gloves and spread a linen square over her lap to protect herself from ink stains) and then announcing that we would be having lunch a bit early because of the Mets game. She loved the Mets, then owned by her cousin Joan Payson, and was a great fan of Tom Seaver. Toward the end, I remember the difficulty with which she walked and the pleasure she got from a playful cane Lev gave her, designed like a fishing rod, with a reel near the handle. I remember her delight when her daughter Pam LeBoutillier decided to renovate and move into Gertrude's Old Westbury studio, and I remember the fun we all had at Pam's "How You'd Like To Be Remembered" house-warming costume party. . . .

This past year I was again about to write a birthday letter when Flora Biddle called to say her mother had died. I hated writing a letter of condolence instead. I hated the thought of never again seeing Flora Miller.

B.H. Friedman was a Trustee of the Whitney Museum of American Art (1961–78) and has since then been an Honorary Trustee. He is the author of Gertrude Vanderbilt Whitney, *a biography with the research collaboration of Flora Miller Biddle. In addition to six novels and a collection of stories, he has published works on Lee Krasner, Alfonso Ossorio, Jackson Pollock, Salvatore Scarpitta, and Myron Stout.*

Above: Flora at retirement party for Chief Security Guard, Sylone Brown (in striped tie), June 1978. Mr. Brown was an employee of the Whitney Museum of American Art from 1939 to 1978, and Flora made a special effort to be present at the party to commend him for his loyal service. Behind Flora and Mr. Brown are members of the security staff (from left): Dell Holder, Jr., Ronald E. Langley, and Mr. Brown's successor, Altamont Fairclough.

Right: Flora in one of her customary pantsuits with Norborne Berkeley, Jr. (left), Trustee of the Whitney Museum of American Art (1976–82), and her son-in-law Michael H. Irving, Trustee (1961–80), consulting architect with Marcel Breuer of the Whitney Museum of American Art at Madison Avenue and Seventy-fifth Street, and currently Honorary Trustee; September 1973.

Left: Drawing of Flora and her younger sister Barbara Whitney (left) by Aimé Morot, 1910, pastel on paper.

Below: James Earle Fraser, *Flora and Sonny-Boy Whitney*, 1907, pewter relief, installed in the sun porch of Flora's home in Old Westbury.

Growing Up

Cornelius Vanderbilt Whitney
Gertrude Conner
Betsey Whitney
Sandra Payson

Flora and her brother Sonny (Cornelius Vanderbilt) Whitney at the wedding of Helen Barney and Archibald Alexander, April 8, 1905.

Although there were three of us—Flora, Barbara, and me—my closest association was with my sister Flora. I remember our early years playing together in Old Westbury, riding our ponies and sledding down the hills. Flora had a French governess and I a tutor, and it was because of Flora's governess that I learned fluent French at an early age. We both had great respect for our mother, who used to spend many hours in her studio sculpting. I can even remember Flora trying to model in clay.

Flora was a devoted sister and playmate. I remember her coming-out years in New York and Newport, and even though I was two years younger, I was asked by my family to escort her to her parties. Needless to say, she was always the most popular of the débutantes and we were all terribly excited when my father had a ballroom built in Newport for her coming-out party there.

Flora and I, because of Mama, took a special interest in American art and were often exposed to the young artists and their works. We worked together after the death of our mother to carry out her plans and ideals for the Whitney Museum. When so many business activities controlled my life and when I found that I did not have enough time to spend working actively for the Museum, I resigned and my sister Flora did an outstanding job of making the Museum today one of which our mother would be proud.

Our thoughts and ideals have been similar throughout the years, and it is our early childhood and growing up together and often talking about our ambitions and dreams that have helped both of us to achieve so many things in our lifetimes. Flora always backed me, either morally or financially, in my various ventures. She was most enthusiastic about Marineland Florida, when I helped to establish it in 1936, and was one of the stockholders, and she invested in Pioneer Pictures, my motion picture company that produced *Gone with the Wind*.

Even though my sister Flora is no longer with us, her work and dreams for the Whitney Museum and my fond memories of her will live on forever.

Cornelius Vanderbilt Whitney

Flora P. Whitney & Sells Whitney

Jack

Although their paths seldom crossed, my mother and my aunt Flora were bound by many threads. Whenever my mother was in some serious difficulty, my aunt would rally to her side. A typical example is the time my mother was ill in the hospital and my aunt (herself also ailing) went right to her bedside in a wheelchair—to be with her and comfort her.

Gertrude Conner

My mother, Joan Whitney Payson, had grown up with her cousin Flora Miller, and they spent many happy times together in the Adirondacks and in Lenox, Massachusetts. There were many photos in the family album of the two of them, usually in enormous hats and no shoes. There was deep family feeling and great affection, and this was transmitted to the next generation.

Sandra Payson

How can one say enough about Flora Miller? I loved her and found her one of the most enchanting people I've ever known and I know that Jock felt the same way.

Betsey Whitney

Right: Flora, seated between her cousins Jock (John Hay) and Joan Whitney, c. 1903.

Facing page: Album page with photographs of Flora and her cousin Jock (John Hay) Whitney at Camp Deerlands in the Adirondacks, c. 1913. Camp Deerlands on Little Forked Lake is one of many separate rustic camps built throughout the Whitney property which originally covered approximately 100,000 acres of forests, mountains, and lakes.

Gertrude Vanderbilt and Harry Payne Whitney had three children, Flora Payne Whitney (1897–1986), Cornelius Vanderbilt (Sonny) Whitney (b. 1899), and Barbara Whitney (1903–1983).

Flora's first cousins, John Hay (Jock) Whitney and Joan Whitney (later Mrs. Charles Shipman Payson), were the children of Harry's younger brother (William) Payne Whitney and his wife, Helen Hay Whitney.

Gertrude (Mrs. McCauley) Conner is the daughter of Barbara Whitney and her first husband, Barklie McKee Henry. She is a Trustee of the Skowhegan School of Painting and Sculpture.

Betsey Cushing (Mrs. John Hay) Whitney is the widow of Jock Whitney. In addition to many philanthropic activities, she is a member of the Jockey Club, an Honorary Life Governor of New York Hospital, and an Honorary Trustee of Yale University Medical Library.

Sandra Payson is the daughter of Joan Whitney and Charles Shipman Payson and was a Trustee of the Whitney Museum of American Art (1975–85).

Of Great Houses

Brendan Gill

We speak with envy of the *douceur de vivre* enjoyed by members of society in the days when Flora Whitney Miller was young, but we do well to recall that the phrase implies not sweetness but ease. Though we can speculate with some confidence on how much easier it may have been for a certain class of people to have lived at a certain time, we must be wary of describing the emotions they entertained in the presence of that ease. Questions of feeling are hard to document; take, for example, happiness, which hovers in the background of most of our speculations about the past: who is to say what it is, much less whether anyone has been fortunate enough to experience it? Marcus Aurelius said that even in a palace life can be lived well, and the statement is a witty one in part because we perceive (reluctantly, standing outside the palace gates) that even in a palace life can be lived badly. Be that as it may, and with the proviso that what we are discussing here is not happiness but comfort, I think it is safe to say that all those young Vanderbilts and Whitneys, as they moved in their mock-royal progresses from great house to great house according to season, were indeed sharing a degree of luxury unknown to ordinary mortals, then or now.

Those great houses did not happen by chance. The Vanderbilts and the Whitneys commanded the services of the best architects of their time—George Post, Richard Morris Hunt, Stanford White, William Adams Delano—to provide them not merely with shelter but with outward and visible signs of their newfound high place in the world. Money talks and sometimes money shouts, but the most cultivated voice that money possesses is the silent one of architecture. It is also the most convincing. On Fifth Avenue at the turn of the century the Vanderbilts signaled their financial superiority so convincingly with town house after town house that the Astors, hitherto imperturbably aloof, had to make haste to keep up with them. Nor were the Whitneys far behind; when Gertrude Vanderbilt left her parents' block long red-brick French château on Fifth Avenue between Fifty-seventh and Fifty-eighth Streets to marry Harry Payne Whitney, her life was not much expanded in geographical terms.

Left: The Fifth Avenue mansion of Flora's maternal grandparents, Cornelius and Alice Gwynne Vanderbilt at 1 West Fifty-seventh Street. Originally occupying only the corner of the site, the house was remodeled and enlarged beginning in 1892 under the supervision of architect George B. Post to occupy the entire block between Fifty-seventh and Fifty-eighth Streets. This view, from the northeast corner of Fifth Avenue and Fifty-eighth Street, shows the monumental gate and fence which Gertrude Vanderbilt Whitney subsequently gave to the City of New York; they now serve as the entrance to the Rose Garden in Central Park at Fifth Avenue and One Hundred and Fifth Street.

Facing page: Marble mantelpiece by Augustus Saint-Gaudens with mosaic designed by John La Farge in the main hall of 1 West Fifty-seventh Street. The mantelpiece is presently in the collection of the Metropolitan Museum of Art, Gift of Mrs. Cornelius Vanderbilt, Sr., 1925. At the time of the gift, the life-size caryatids were not transferred to the Metropolitan Museum. They were discovered in 1978 in the garden of Gertrude Vanderbilt Whitney's studio in Old Westbury and subsequently given to the Metropolitan Museum by Flora. The entire mantelpiece is now installed in the Charles Engelhard Court of the American Wing.

Facing page, top: 871 Fifth Avenue, c. 1940. When William C. Whitney died in 1904, his home at 871 Fifth Avenue was sold, along with its entire contents. In 1909, the new owner died and Harry, not wishing a great family legacy to be dispersed at auction bought the fifty-four-room house and over 914 catalogued items of art, furniture, and furnishings which had belonged to his father. Flora lived in this, her second home, from 1910 until her first marriage in 1920.

Facing page, lower left: Main hall of 871 Fifth Avenue, interiors designed by Stanford White of the architectural firm McKim, Mead and White. The elaborate redecorating of the interior of 871 Fifth Avenue began in 1897 and was completed in 1902, just two years before William C. Whitney's death. Two of the Gobelin tapestries from the house, *Air, Juno* and *Autumn, Bacchus,* are now in the collection of the Cleveland Museum of Art.

Facing page, lower right: Dining room of 871 Fifth Avenue, designed by Stanford White. As described in the catalogue prepared in 1909 for the auction of "The Palatial Mansion and Its Exceedingly Rare and Costly Artistic Furnishings and Embellishments" (published in B. H. Friedman, *Gertrude Vanderbilt Whitney,* 1978):

"The three interior walls [of the dining room] are entirely covered, from baseboard to ceiling, with old Italian paintings. Toned with age, these paintings constitute a unique decoration for a New York interior, and the room easily ranks among the most notable in this very notable mansion. The paintings are on canvas, applied to the walls, and include innumerable figures wearing the costumes of many nations.

The entrance doorway from the Main Hall is provided with a monumental frame, gilded in every part and known as the Golden Doorway. . . . The entablature has a frieze of scrolls and arabesques, and on the summit is the lion of St. Mark.

Above: 2 West Fifty-seventh Street was the first residence of the infant Flora. It was the home of her paternal grandfather, William C. Whitney, who gave it to the newly married Harry and Gertrude Vanderbilt Whitney in 1896 when he moved to 871 Fifth Avenue.

The ceiling was brought from a palace in Genoa. It is of the coffered type. . . . The whole is surrounded with an outer border of arabesques on a blue ground.

The mantel, in the centre of the north wall, is one of the most interesting in the Mansion. It is a beautiful antique of Fiesole stone. The hollow curve of the facing has a small diaper of fleur-de-lis, and slender columns on decorated bases support consoles that carry the overmantel. . . . The large central panel above contains a representation of a fight on a bridge and includes a number of figures in high relief. . . . Over all is a plain slab applied directly to the wall, on which are three shields. All of this beautiful structure was once picked out with gold, much of which is still visible."

The young couple soon took over the house at 2 West Fifty-seventh Street that had belonged to Harry's father, William C. Whitney, a widower who, upon his remarriage, set about the remodeling, under Stanford White's direction, of a mansion of fifty-odd rooms at 871 Fifth Avenue. A few years later, when old William C. died, Harry with filial piety and to Gertrude's displeasure insisted upon moving into 871. It was White who designed the Whitneys' country place in Old Westbury, in which Flora Whitney Miller grew up. (Of the many buildings that White designed for the estate, only the water tower, one of his most attractive works, remains standing.) Later, Gertrude Whitney called upon "Billy" Delano to design a studio for her in neo-Renaissance style, set in a garden that might just as readily have been hidden among the green umbrella pines of Tuscany as among the somewhat less umbrella-like pines of Long Island. All those big houses to move among as fashion dictated—New York, Old Westbury, Saratoga, the Adirondacks, Newport, Palm Beach! Who but an ignorant outsider can have dared to invent the phrase "the idle rich"? The rich worked hard and long at their pleasures and upon their cultural tasks as well, being as time passed more and more often pressed into service on behalf of museums, schools, hospitals, and a host of other worthy charitable causes. The days of innumerable servants passed and so, little by little, did a number of the houses, some of them being thrown down and others being devoted to new and mildly ironic purposes (a ballroom becomes a chapel, a chapel becomes a squash court, a squash court becomes an office). Many of the great houses in which Flora Whitney Miller lived have vanished without a trace. We can measure the loss of them in architectural terms; in other terms, sound judgments are difficult to make. For vanished houses, like most vanished things, take on the romance of a past that, simply by being the past, may be thought to have been filled with wonders. We have only to utter the magical words, "Once upon a time," and all things become possible.

Brendan Gill

Brendan Gill, author and critic for The New Yorker, *has been a Trustee of the Whitney Museum of American Art since 1979. He was recently selected to revive "The Sky Line" architecture column in* The New Yorker, *which was last written by Lewis Mumford. In addition to numerous books and plays, he is the author of* Here at The New Yorker *and a soon to be published biography of Frank Lloyd Wright.*

Left: Water tower designed by Stanford White in Old Westbury. It is the only structure that remains of the buildings White designed for William C. Whitney on the Old Westbury estate.

Facing page: Gertrude Vanderbilt Whitney's studio in Old Westbury, designed by William Adams Delano, 1910–13, now the home of Flora's daughter, Pamela T. LeBoutillier. The fountain was designed by Gertrude Vanderbilt Whitney and a cast was in the foyer of the first Whitney Museum of American Art, 10 West Eighth Street.

Following spread, left page: Album page with photographs of Gertrude Vanderbilt and Harry Payne Whitney's estate in Old Westbury, 1916. The landscape architects Olmsted, Elliott and Olmsted supervised the landscaping of the seven hundred-acre property of woods and meadows, which originally belonged to Flora's paternal grandfather, William C. Whitney, and Stanford White designed the main house.

Following spread, right page: Album page with photographs of Camp Deerlands in the Adirondacks, c. 1935. Camp Deerlands was originally built by Flora's grandfather, William C. Whitney, in the late nineteenth century, and is still used by Flora's brother, Cornelius Vanderbilt (Sonny) Whitney, and his family.

Westbury   1914

Westbury   1914

The Tennis-court.   1914

Gymnasium.   1914

Westbury.   1914

The Breakers

Facing page: Album page with photograph of "The Breakers," designed by Richard Morris Hunt and completed in 1895. This was the Newport residence of Flora's maternal grandparents, Cornelius and Alice Gwynne Vanderbilt.

Top of page: Aerial view of "The Breakers."

Bottom of page: Great hall of "The Breakers."

Daughter of a Brilliant Mother

Beatrice Straight

Flora Miller was a very exceptional person. Growing up as she did in a world of great wealth and to say the least a somewhat eccentric world, she might have been overwhelmed by those around her. But she was encouraged by her brilliant mother Gertrude Vanderbilt Whitney, whom she adored, to develop into an amazing woman in her own right, a woman of great purpose and style. She combined the qualities of warmth and openness, a fine sense of humor, plus the ability to carry through to conclusion such a vast and demanding undertaking as the developing of the Whitney Museum of American Art, at the same time raising a lovely family. She had the vision and strength, the business acumen to continue working for the growth of all these things she loved.

My personal memory of her will always be with me. Her warm and generous spirit, her rich loving laughter. All this and more. It was a joy to have known her.

Beatrice Straight, Flora's cousin, is an Academy Award-winning actress and the daughter of Harry Payne Whitney's sister, Dorothy, and Willard Straight. Young Beatrice and her brother Whitney were members of the wedding party when Flora married Roderick Tower in 1920.

me diary by stunt!

Above: Flora at Camp Deerlands, in the Adirondacks, c. 1913 (notation by Flora).

Right: Flora at Camp Deerlands, c. 1926—the photograph of his wife that G. Macculloch Miller kept always on his desk.

Facing page: Jo Davidson, *Flora*, 1909, bronze. Jo Davidson went to Paris in 1908 when he was twenty-five and met Gertrude Vanderbilt Whitney, who commissioned this bust of Flora. In 1916 he returned to the United States and Gertrude assisted him in securing a studio in MacDougal Alley. Jo and his wife, Yvonne, later became lifelong friends of Flora and witnessed her marriage to G. Macculloch Miller in Cairo in 1927.

Gertrude Vanderbilt Whitney, extraordinary personality of an eccentric world, depicted by four artists in the costume designed for her by Leon Bakst: Baron de Meyer, photograph, c. 1913, collection of Pamela T. LeBoutillier; Emanuele de Rosales, silver statuette, c. 1913; Howard Cushing, mural, c. 1915, oil on canvas, second floor landing, Old Westbury studio; John Singer Sargent, drawing, c. 1913, pencil on paper.

Daughter of an International Star

Devereux Milburn, Jr.

In the polo world in the first quarter of this century, my father's friend Harry Payne Whitney was lord of all he surveyed, and his daughter, Flora, lived in his heaven. Flora, an irrepressible romantic all her life, was in her element. I do not have to imagine this— she told me so many, many times.

In 1886, an English polo team visited Newport and defeated the Americans for the newly established Westchester Cup. The Americans failed to regain it in 1902 in England. It must have been shortly thereafter that Harry Payne Whitney decided to take matters in hand and to devote his leadership, his skill, his time, and, last but not least, his money to recapturing and retaining the Cup.

He began by acquiring the finest string of polo ponies ever collected, which he kept at the famous Whitney Stable in Old Westbury, the largest privately owned stable in the world. I have been told on very reliable authority that in International years, Mr. Whitney owned one hundred and fifty ponies: fifty for the team to play in important matches, fifty for practice matches and reserves, and fifty turned out for rest and rehabilitation.

Newspaper photograph of Flora's father, Harry Payne Whitney, which Flora kept framed in her bedroom in Old Westbury. The caption beneath the photograph, c. 1913, reads: "A Leader of American Sport. Captain Harry Payne Whitney, who will lead the American polo team into action next week, when they clash with the British challengers, in an effort to retain that famous international trophy, the Hurlingham Cup. This cup was brought to the United States in 1909 by an American team under the leadership of Captain Whitney, and successfully defended by a team under his captaincy in 1911."

AMERICA'S VICTORY OVER ENGLAND AT POLO FOR THE "AMERICA" CUP

The American Invasion Was Brought to a Successful Conclusion by Victories at Hurlingham. All Leading Polo Authorities of England Agree That the Meadow Brook Team Was the Best Ever Seen In That Country.

THE AMERICAN POLO TEAM.
(From Left to Right)
Devereux Milburn, H. P. Whitney, J. M. Waterbury, Lawrence Waterbury.

THE FIRST GAME AT HURLINGHAM, Receiving a Throw-In, An English Player (Dark Shirt) About to Strike the Ball.

H. P. WHITNEY (Rider on Right) Just After Scoring a Goal.

THE CUP WHICH IS COMING BACK.

A Few of the American Ponies Out For Exercise. More Than 100 Were Taken To England.

PLAY FROM A THROW-IN.

Devereux Milburn (in white) Riding Off An English Opponent.

LAWRENCE WATERBURY.

(Photo by Underwood & Underwood, N. Y.)

SPECTATORS AT HURLINGHAM.

The next step was to assemble the team. However much interest Flora may have had in the ponies, I am sure they took a back seat in her heart to the players. Many of them lived in her father's house, at least during the polo season. Polo has always been a young man's game, and the "squad" from which Mr. Whitney selected his final "Big Four" numbered at least twenty. Picture, therefore, this young girl, extremely romantic and imaginative, living in this exciting world. She used to tell me of the almost unbearable crushes she suffered through year after year.

The Americans won the Cup in 1909, 1911 and 1913 with the same team, captained, of course, by Harry Payne Whitney. He was the non-playing captain in 1914 and again the power behind the successful invasion of England in 1921.

All these years of growing up, Flora was the queen of this kingdom. Much of her mother's time was devoted to her artistic and philanthropic interests, and polo was of very secondary importance. Flora was her father's constant companion. I can never forget how her face lit up and her eyes sparkled when so often we talked about those glorious days.

Devereux Milburn, Jr. is the son of Harry Payne Whitney's teammate, Devereux Milburn, and is senior partner of Carter, Ledyard & Milburn. He was legal counsel to Flora for many years.

Facing page: Page from *The New York Times,* Sunday, July 18, 1909. Photo story reporting the victory of Harry Payne Whitney and his polo team for the "America Cup."

Left: Flora seated between her mother, Gertrude Vanderbilt Whitney, and her younger sister Barbara at a polo match, c. 1913.

Below: Herbert Haseltine, *Meadowbrook Team,* 1909, bronze, collection of the Whitney Museum of American Art. Commissioned by Harry Payne Whitney the year his Meadowbrook polo team won the "America Cup." Depicted from left: Devereux Milburn on "The Roan Mare," Lawrence Waterbury on "Little Mary," Harry Payne Whitney on "Cotton Tail," and J. Montgomery (Monty) Waterbury on "Cobnut." Haseltine was a friend of Harry and Gertrude Vanderbilt Whitney and the most noted sculptor of equestrian subjects of his time.

Thoroughbreds

Whitney Tower

Although Ma was not, in the strictest sense of the word, a horsewoman, few young American ladies could match her childhood, marked by an atmosphere which literally reeked of horses of varied breeds. There was a lot more talk of polo than of dollhouses around the Old Westbury and Aiken estates. There were, in fact, many horses to talk about: those for horse shows in Aiken, drag-hunting mounts and some used purely for the leisurely driving of buggies through Aiken's beautiful Hitchcock Woods.

But while her father Harry, her brother Sonny, and her devoted cousin Jock were deeply involved in the world of club, national, and international polo—a world which was also a focal point of interest for the parents of many of her close friends—it was an even larger world, that of thoroughbred racing, which was of paramount importance in the Whitney family. Ma's grandfather, William C. Whitney, one of the pioneers who had helped bring respectability to Saratoga racing at the turn of the century, laid the foundation for the Whitney Stud and its incredible success on tracks in the U.S. and, to some extent, in England as well.

Harry Payne Whitney not only carried on this tradition, he managed to strengthen its prestige before passing on the Eton blue and brown silks to his son C.V. (Sonny) Whitney. Those familiar colors now belong to my brother Lev Miller who, with his wife Linda, operates T-Square Stud in Fairfield, Florida.

Below: Rosa Bonheur, *The Horse Fair*, 1853–55, oil on canvas, collection of the Metropolitan Museum of Art, Gift of Cornelius Vanderbilt, 1887. Cornelius Vanderbilt, Flora's maternal grandfather, was a Trustee of the Metropolitan Museum (1878–99) and Chairman of its Executive Committee. Later, Flora's brother Cornelius Vanderbilt (Sonny) Whitney was a Trustee of the Metropolitan Museum (1943–47).

Facing page: "Regret" in the Winner's Circle, Kentucky Derby, Churchill Downs, Louisville, Kentucky, 1915. Although Whitney-owned and bred thoroughbreds had been making headlines since before the turn of the century, a major milestone of national acclaim was reached in 1915 when the filly "Regret," owned by Flora's father, Harry Payne Whitney, became the first of her sex to win the Kentucky Derby. It was another sixty-five years before another filly, "Genuine Risk," duplicated the feat in 1980.

Cousins too were heavily involved with racing. Jock Whitney and his sister Joan Payson took over their mother's Greentree Stable, while another cousin, Alfred Gwynne Vanderbilt, was highly successful in his own right. The names of winners discussed in the many Whitney drawing rooms read like a Who's Who of Racing. In 1901, W.C.'s "Volodyovski" captured the Derby at Epsom. After a successful career on the British turf, Harry's "Whisk Broom II" won the 1913 Handicap Triple Crown in New York, and two years later his "Regret" became the first filly to win the Kentucky Derby (H.P.W. won a second Derby with "Whiskery" in 1927). Appropriately named "Upset" handed "Man o' War" his sole defeat in the 1919 Sanford Stakes at Saratoga.

Additional racing glory came to the Whitneys through the exploits of, among others, "John P. Grier," "Equipoise," "Twenty Grand," "Devil Diver," "Tom Fool," and steeplechaser "Jolly Roger." Cousin Alfred Vanderbilt kept pace with his celebrated "Native Dancer," and from the earliest days of this thoroughbred empire the family's record of breeding champions matched the successes achieved on the nation's tracks.

Ma's participation in racing was not what you'd call passionately intense. She did visit Saratoga occasionally. In fact, as a young lady often accompanied by her closest friend Helen Hitchcock, she visited her father at Cady Hill, the Whitney summer house which was regarded, during the racing season, as a smoke-filled bachelor's pad and the permanent site of heralded high-stakes poker games. So well did Ma learn her poker lessons at Harry's table that later in life she

was often the only lady invited to traditional men's games in New York.

Her subsequent visits to Saratoga were mainly to visit Sonny or Jock and take in a little gambling at the old clubs, which were put out of business in the 1950s. After one such escapade, she was persuaded to attend the yearling sales where, for reasons she never could explain, she found herself the high-bidder on a filly which she promptly named "Spa Madness." Ma's final association with Saratoga was to take an absentee interest in my involvement with the National Museum of Racing. She was equally aware of Lev's horse business in Florida, much as she had been interested some years ago in his jumpers at Belmont Park and before that when Pam was racing "The Doge," once the star performer of her Pentagon Stable.

In later years Ma attended many of Lev's polo games as well as granddaughter Susi Humes' horse show appearances. As for the thoroughbreds, her interest reached its annual peak as she sat by her television set during the Triple Crown races. On these exciting occasions she could be counted upon to supervise the $10 pools. I was never in on that action, but those who were regulars had one common recollection: it was strictly cash you tossed in the pot. No credit allowed!

Whitney Tower, son of Flora and Roderick Tower, is an internationally known sportswriter and the President of the National Museum of Racing, Inc. in Saratoga Springs, New York.

Left: Cady Hill House, Saratoga Springs, New York. Owned by Flora's father, Harry Payne Whitney, and now owned by her brother, Cornelius Vanderbilt (Sonny) Whitney.

Below: Flora's thoroughbred, "Spa Madness," 1937 (notation by Cully).

Facing page: Flora, the young equestrian, taking a fence on her jumper in Aiken, c. 1917.

F.W.M's ONE AND ONLY (SO FAR) RACE HORSE —
"SPA--MADNESS"

Foxcroft

Nancy Perkins Lancaster

I *loved* Flora—we roomed together at Foxcroft and she was my maid of honor when I married Henry Field. She was one of the few people I've known who had *real* charm (the rarest of gifts, and very different from attraction, which often does not bring happiness). The last time I saw her she came to take me to see Helen Clark and except for a walking stick and trousers, she looked exactly the same as always—those lovely eyes and that "fluted" mouth I always teased her about. How I like to remember her is being in one of the Foxcroft open wooden classrooms with golf stockings on (for the cold) and ballet shoes as she practiced "toe standing" from her chair during lessons. She had the most lovely disposition. The year we came out I stayed at Newport for "her Ball"—and her father gave me a lovely dress from Hollanders. We danced till sunrise and bathed in the ocean. (A very advanced thing to do then but hardly to be mentioned now.) I did see her at Hobe Sound—when she heard of my arrival, she (ever thoughtful) had my cottage filled with food. I wish our paths had crossed oftener—but her memory and the real affection I felt for her never lessen—

I feel I am the last leaf on the tree as our class at Foxcroft is now not even mentioned and no wonder as I am the sole survivor—

Nancy Perkins Lancaster was born in September 1897 in Charlottesville, Virginia. Her mother was one of the Langhorne sisters from Charlottesville, famous for their great beauty and the gracious life they led at their home, "Mirador." Nancy Perkins married Henry Field in 1917; he died five months later. In 1920 she married Ronald Tree and had three children. The Trees were divorced in the early 1940s, and she married Claude G. Lancaster in the 1950s. During World War II, Winston Churchill came to spend weekends at her house, "Dytcheley"—"if there was a bright moon! It was a better place to hide from the German planes."

Flora entered Foxcroft in Middleburg, Virginia, in September 1914, and was a member of the first graduating class. At Foxcroft she and Nancy Perkins (Lancaster) were classmates and great friends. Flora's daughter Pamela T. LeBoutillier recently visited Mrs. Lancaster in Oxford, England, and reported: "When Nancy's legs were sore from exercising, Flora took all the lavender water from the whole school and rubbed it into them! They smoked pipes with 'rabbit tobacco' in the Pink House where they lived with Martha Williams from Charleston as the third roommate and Miss Ida Appleton as chaperone." In later years, Flora remembered that she and her roommates slept on sleeping porches and sometimes could hear men leaving a nearby tavern loudly whispering, "Be quiet, we mustn't wake the young ladies."

Facing page: Album page with photographs of Foxcroft. Persons identified include: Miss Charlotte (Charlotte Noland), Headmistress; Miss Ida (Ida Appleton), chaperone of Pink House where Flora lived; Flora's roommate Nancy Perkins (Lancaster) and other friends assembled on the porch of Pink House and posing for photographs on the grounds of Foxcroft.

Foxcroft 1914 + 1915

Alice myself

Miss Ida

Miss Charlotte

Nancy

Nancy "Buddy"

Mary "Tommy" Nancy Anne "Kitty"

Mary "Ships" "Anny" Betty - Martha

Early Social Service

William P.T. Preston

Flora and my mother, Fan, were such close friends and so simpatico—almost interchangeable in their stylish élan and spirited confrontation of life. They lived and loved well, zestfully and deeply, and enjoyed the narratives of life they each created. And they each had a very special laugh, the sign of the joy and amusement they felt at the manifestations of human foibles and triumphs.

Each was a sterling character and old-fashioned in carrying forward the values of an earlier generation. With each, one felt in touch with a glorious and fun-filled past. And they danced and sang their way through life as though it were a Broadway musical. They each had the lyric attitude.

I speak of them as one because they always seemed part of a duet, and Fan's earlier death ended their lovely partnership. Flora was also wonderfully generous to Fan in all possible ways.

I am thankful that that generosity, spirit and humor live on in Flora's children, for in this way both Fan and Aunt Flora remain close to us all—resonating now in the music their children create.

William P.T. Preston is the son of one of Flora's best friends, Fanny Baldwin Morgan Preston. He is Professor Emeritus, John Jay College of Criminal Justice, New York City, where he taught American history.

Below, left: During World War I, Flora joined others in the war effort. The caption to this photograph, which appeared in *Vogue*, December 15, 1918, with Flora second from the right and William P.T. Preston's mother, Fanny Baldwin, at the far right, stated: "These are some of the Junior League girls who sold Y pies for the Y.M.C.A. Fund during the United War Work campaign. Reading from left to right, are: Miss Edith Pratt, Miss Louise Butler, Mrs. McLelland, Miss Helen Pratt, Mrs. Francis Rogers, Miss Katherine Emmett, Miss Helen James, Miss Flora Whitney, and Miss Fanny Baldwin. They sold Y pies during the United War Work campaign at the Ritz, Sherry's, Delmonico's, and the Plaza. These pies were very popular desserts from November eleventh to November eighteenth."

Below, right: Flora (second from left) and other ladies, including Alice Davison (second from right), who served in the Red Cross during World War I.

Facing page: Album page of newspaper clippings showing Flora at a typewriter in the office of the Chairman of the National Executive Committee, Republican Women's Headquarters, Washington, D.C., and (from left): Mrs. George W. Reinecke, executive secretary, unidentified individual, Flora, and Mrs. Medill McCormick, Chairman of the Committee, 1919. As a young lady, Flora was anxious to make a personal contribution to social causes. This was recorded by the newspapers in 1919 when she was working in Washington, D.C. with headlines such as "Heiress to Whitney Millions Can Make Own Living at 20."

MISS FLORA PAYNE WHITNEY

Miss Whitney, twenty-year-old daughter of Harry Payne Whitney, of New York, is secretary and assistant to Mrs. Medill McCormick, Chairman of the Republican Women's National Executive Committee.

Heiress to Whitney Millions Can Make Own Living at 20

MISS FLORA
PAYNE
WHITNEY
©HARRIS AND
EWING

Miss Flora Payne Whitney, twenty-year-old daughter of Harry Payne Whitney, New York millionaire sportsman, learned typewriting in the hope of doing Red Cross or Y. M. C. A. work overseas. When the war left her flat (for something to do, not for money) she went to work at the headquarters of the Women's Republican National Executive Committee as volunteer Secretary and assistant to Mrs. McCormick.

The sign on the door tells what the place is. At the left is Mrs. George W. Reinecke, executive secretary; standing is Miss Flora Payne Whitney, volunteer secretary to the chairman, and at the right is Mrs. Medill McCormick, wife of the Senator from Illinois, chairman of the committee. The organization is very active and the sponsors are confident of its success.

Copyright Harris

First Born

Pamela T. LeBoutillier

This is Mum looking terribly surprised to see
that she's produced a baby!! Me!!

Mum was the very *best* Grey Lady at the Mitchell Field Hospital during World War II. We worked the same shifts sometimes to save gas. I was a nurse's aide, but could see her in action at times! *All* the wounded soldiers wanted *her* to read to them or write their loved ones a letter.

Facing page: Flora and her first child, Pamela Tower (LeBoutillier). Flora and her husband, Roderick Tower, were living in Los Angeles at the time of Pamela's birth in 1921. The *San Francisco Examiner* reported the event with the headline, "Mrs. Whitney Now A Grandmother; Baby Girl Will Inherit Millions."

Above: Flora and her daughter Pamela in their uniforms as volunteer hospital workers during World War II.

Pamela Tower LeBoutillier, daughter of Flora and Roderick Tower, has been a volunteer at the American Museum of Natural History for many years, continuing a family tradition of patronage and support of that institution which began with her great-grandfather, William C. Whitney, who was a Trustee of that museum (1891–1900). Her grandmother, Gertrude Vanderbilt Whitney, served on the committee of the scientific staff (1930–34). Her uncle Sonny (Cornelius Vanderbilt Whitney) was a Trustee (1930–60) and an Honorary Trustee (1960–61), and served on the special committee for the Whitney Memorial building between 1931 and 1934. The Whitney family support is commemorated by busts of William C. Whitney and Harry Payne Whitney in the hall named for them. The inscription on the accompanying plaque reads as follows:

> *William C. Whitney (1841–1904) was patron of the American Museum expeditions to the western United States in search of fossil ancestors of the horse.*
>
> *Harry Payne Whitney (1872–1930), his son, supported for fifteen years the Whitney South Seas Expedition in the schooner* France, *which obtained unique collections of Pacific Island birds, examples of which are displayed in this hall. In conjunction with the City of New York, he also built this wing of the Museum to house its department of birds.*
>
> *Gertrude Vanderbilt Whitney (1875–1942), wife of Harry Payne Whitney, together with her three children, presented to the Museum the Rothschild Collection, numbering 280,000 specimens of birds of the world, and established this exhibition hall in memory of her husband and his father.*
>
> *On behalf of the citizens of New York, the Trustees of the Museum gratefully acknowledge these and other notable gifts from this family, extending over a period of fifty years.*

Marriage to G. Macculloch Miller

Flora Miller Biddle
Pamela T. LeBoutillier

Top left: Flora and Cully at Aiken, c. 1940.

Center left: Flora and Cully at the 1939 World's Fair, New York City.

Lower left: Flora and Cully at the reception following the marriage of Pamela Tower and her first husband, Jay K. Secor, at Aiken on December 20, 1941.

Facing page: Cully intent on producing a watercolor drawing, a profession which occupied him increasingly as he grew older, c. 1970.

Sitting at the desk he inherited from his Murray (of Murray Hill) ancestors, I recall my father's quiet pride in his forebears, with their deep roots in America—he talked of Hoffmans, Lindleys, Ogdens, and Maccullochs, and made sure my brother Leverett and I met our two great aunts, his oldest surviving relatives. One, Edith Macculloch Miller, left me "one of my pins given to my great-great-aunt, Miss Murray, by General Washington, set in pearls and with his hair . . ." (the mystery of *that* couple still lingers).

My father grew up in New York with his parents, Hoffman and Edith McKeever Miller, often visiting his grandparents in Morristown, New Jersey, where they lived in Macculloch Hall. In the family tradition, he attended St. Paul's School in Concord, New Hampshire. There he had a "bully time," as his letters home attest, singing in choirs and concerts with his two brothers and making many close lifelong friends. Later at the Art Students League, he developed the talent for drawing and painting which brought him and many others great joy all his life.

G. Macculloch Miller and Flora Tower were an enchanting couple in the mid-1920s —picture a handsome, debonair bachelor of forty and a slim, lovely flapper. Their cruise in a *dahabeah* (a double-decker barge) on the Nile in 1927 and, subsequently, their romantic wedding in Cairo, signaled a life filled with exotic places, people and events; and from their children's perspective, it certainly was.

"Cully," then working for his uncle's MM Importing Co., was charming and elegant in endless ways—as befits a man born on New Year's Eve! His clothes were tailored to perfection, and in very much his style; he was the first man I remember seeing in double-breasted jackets, and even in fishing and hunting outfits he looked better than anyone. He played games very well, bridge almost professionally. His use of language was meticulous—how he hated "drapes" instead of curtains! And when I called a basin a "sink," he made a cogently satiric watercolor to chastise me gently. He drank carefully measured martinis—only the driest—and cared greatly about good wine, good food—at "Duck Soup" near Charleston, he would make sure his canvasbacks had hung for just long enough, and after roasting them in a blazing oven, he pressed the carcasses in his special silver duck press. Meanwhile, Mum was creating her amazing blue dessert, one of her two or three spectacular culinary accomplishments!

Despite a chronic bad hip, he was an excellent dancer, in the style of his friends Adele and Fred Astaire. His marvelous sense of humor never failed. There were his practical jokes, gentle teasing, his collection of *Jingles by Cully*—for which he used a multitude of experiences, magazine advertisements, letters, people, anything which appealed to his fertile imagination. And just his conversation delighted all who knew him. A partner in the architectural firm of Noel and Miller, he designed objects and buildings which expressed his love of the good life; even his handwriting was stylish.

Above all, he adored our mother totally. Taking her hand, he would turn to me, saying, "Look, my bunch, just see how beautiful she is, not a line on her face" (which was true all her life), and "notice how she *appreciates* everything—that's the greatest quality in life, appreciation." "My bug," he would say to her lovingly, "how are you feeling, how is your tummy"—or "your sniffle" or "your knee." His awareness and care for every detail of her person and her life was extraordinary.

I can picture him vividly; even at the very end of his life his hair was still quite dark, his figure trim, his smile quick—painting, painting, painting, in his armchair after breakfast, on the porch after lunch—painting flowers, or a little fruit, a view from the window, or my mother as she worked on her tapestry or the double-crostic in the *Saturday Review of Literature*.

Flora Miller Biddle

Page from *Jingles by Cully*, a privately printed collection of Cully's verse and drawings published after his death in 1972 as a remembrance of his witty observations on life.

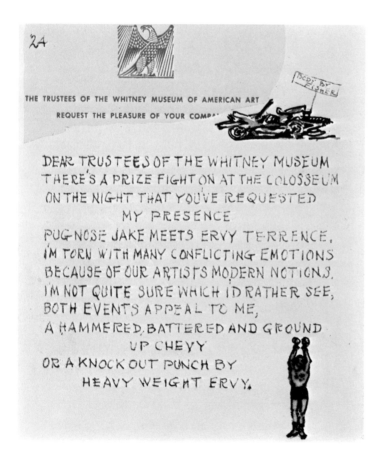

My stepfather Cully Miller spread fun and humor wherever he was—never at the expense of others, but always "hitting the nail on the head." I was very conscious of those "vibes" between my mother and him. They were strong!!! He was just so devoted, patient, and supportive of her that it was a wonder. And, of course, she basked in the luxury of living with someone who gave so much. I feel lucky to have had such a stepparent, as he *never* interfered, except when asked, and gave us all mountains of laughs and fun.

Pamela T. LeBoutillier

Flora Miller Biddle, biographical note, p. 12.
Pamela T. LeBoutillier, biographical note, p. 53.

Mum

Pamela T. LeBoutillier

THE CROWD G.V.W. *Sylvia Leny Flora* TWINS
        Isabric

Above: Flora (standing second from right) and her family gathered at Camp Deerlands in the Adirondacks for her son Leverett S. Miller's fifth birthday party, 1936. Standing at the upper left is Cully, in costume with false mustache, with Whitney Tower on the step below him. Gertrude Vanderbilt Whitney, in hat at center, is surrounded by (clockwise from top): Gloria Vanderbilt, Gertrude Henry (Conner), Pamela Tower (LeBoutillier), Barbara Whitney Henry (Headley), Leverett Miller, and Nancy Whitney (Lutz). On either side of Flora are Cully's nephews, Larry (right) and Cully Miller. Cully's brother, Lawrence Miller (fourth from right), also in costume with false mustache, is seen below Bubby Széchényi (Eltz) and next to Sylvia Széchényi (Szapary), who is above Flora Miller (Biddle), seated on the bottom step.

Following spread: Album page with photographs of Flora and Cully, Gertrude Vanderbilt Whitney, and Flora's children—Pam, Whitty, Flora, and Lev— enjoying themselves as a family.

Growing up Mum's daughter was great fun— never dull. We all moved a lot: in the winter to Aiken, where the boys attended Aiken Preparatory School. But there was no school for the girls at the beginning of our years there. So, Mum and three of her friends started one—in our squash court! They brought a teacher down from the Brearley School so there was a pretty fancy curriculum. This one-room operation was heated by a little wood stove and everyone worked in the same room.

In the spring we moved to New York to the Hotel Pierre for a while—to go to the dentist and the doctor and to buy shoes, as I remember. Then to Old Westbury for a little while before moving us all to Newport to stay with our grandmother, Mrs. Whitney. For August it was the Adirondacks. After that the whole process was repeated backwards, ending up in Aiken again for school!

In the years that we went to France we'd skip Newport, and sometimes even the Adirondacks. This traveling was an intricate business; we took all the dogs, canaries and other pets, such as goats, all the children—we were four—nurses, a maid or two, the chauffeur, the cars. When we went to Aiken we took all the horses and all the household and sometimes ponycarts and buggies. It took a freight car for this, and Loading Day was one of great excitement. We all went down to the station with all our friends and helped cajole and bribe the horses into their right slots in the railway car. One had to be sure each horse had its hay rack within easy reach, etc., etc.

Traveling to and from Europe was even more exciting because of the wonderful five-, six- or seven-day boat trip. The loading of the car was always an event we loved to watch. It looked so tiny swinging around at the end of a crane over the decks or over the water! I guess we were secretly hoping for the big splash—which fortunately never came!

Pamela T. LeBoutillier; biographical note, p. 53.

OUR OUTFIT IN PAGEANT — 100ᵗʰ ANNIVERSARY OF FOUNDING OF AIKEN

G.M.M. & FLORA   PAM

FLORA   LEV.

PAM & FLORA

G.V.W.   Pam   Flora

Lev
on
newfall

HORSE SHOW   Cindy
Flora

PAM   F.W.M. BILL   FLORA   WHIT.

LUNCH ON CAR

FLORA   FWM   WHITTY
LEVI

G.V.W.   Pam   Flora

Lessons to a Son

Leverett S. Miller

Left: G. Macculloch Miller, *Garden House*, 1944, watercolor on paper. Inscribed "To Pam from GMM, May 30, 1944." Cully Miller was an accomplished watercolor artist and made countless sketches of objects and places in his life. He recorded events and beloved scenes for his friends and family.

Facing page: Album page with photographs of Flora and Gertrude Vanderbilt Whitney sitting in the rose garden near the garden house in Old Westbury, c. 1936.

When I think of my mother and the rose garden at the Old Westbury house, I am reminded of so many of her qualities that I hope will pass on to my children.

The garden represented a type of serenity and thoughtfulness. It was ordered, much as she was, with steadfast constancy of purpose and great loyalty to family, marriage, and strong traditional values. The brick paths wandered seemingly aimlessly at times, but always returned to a central focus—the house with the basic foundations of those values. Along with this was the enormous lifelong curiosity about others, about places, about written words, visual images, the mystical, and so much more. These had to be discussed, as my mother is seen doing with her mother and as she did so often with her children, always hoping to instill curiosity, to inspire knowledge and thus respect for others.

The beauty around us may have been incidental at times, but good design and good taste were an integral, if unconscious, part of life in all matters. The example she set for us with her life was the great lesson she had to pass on to all. Like most children, we may have rebelled, but she was the constant to recall us to what was important. She rose to all occasions with great kindness. She rallied us together, as a family, as children, as adults, and so often we didn't realize it.

Leverett S. Miller, son of Flora and G. Macculloch Miller, is a horse breeder living in Fairfield, Florida. He was recently given the Whitney family racing colors of Eton blue and brown by his uncle Sonny (Cornelius Vanderbilt Whitney). The colors were originally those of his great-grandfather, William C. Whitney, who was a founding member of the Jockey Club in 1894.

Sitting in
Garden at her
house that I
have now

G.V.W

F.W.H.   G.V.Whitney

Aiken and Good Times

Seymour H. Knox
Frederick H. von Stade
Ivor G. Balding
Margaret Mellon Hitchcock

Flora and I were friends for many years. We first met when we were in our middle teens, coming back from Europe on a boat with our parents. I, of course, knew Sonny Whitney at Yale and later playing polo.

I did not really get a chance to see Flora until she and Cully moved to Aiken and lived in the old family home. We had wonderful times and over many years. The annual amateur plays coached by Skiddy von Stade were held in Flora's family's home. They were great fun and we all enjoyed them. Flora was a lovely lady and a wonderful hostess. I remember one of the last big parties—she seated me at her right because she had known me longer than anyone else.

The Whitney Museum of American Art was a great interest for Flora and she supported her mother, and the Museum, loyally.

Seymour H. Knox

Left: Aerial view of the Whitney property in Aiken, South Carolina. Flora's grandfather, William C. Whitney, established Aiken as a family place in the late nineteenth century. The focus of the estate was Joye Cottage, described by B.H. Friedman in his biography *Gertrude Vanderbilt Whitney* as "a rambling mansion occupying much of an entire square at the intersection of Easy Street and Whiskey Road (an address which amuses the family), with stables and a squash court on adjoining property." Flora gave the property to her son Whitney Tower, and it has since passed out of the family. The school that Flora established for her children was in the building at the upper left, formerly a squash court.

Facing page, top: Flora leading the parade through Aiken celebrating the 50th anniversary of the founding of polo, accompanied by Devereux Milburn, her father's teammate on the Meadow Brook polo team, 1932.

Facing page, bottom: Amateur theatrical in Aiken. The annual amateur plays coached by Frederick H. (Skiddy) von Stade were held in Flora's family home. Players are (standing from left): Schuyler Parsons, Nancy Bowne McKim, Dunbar Bostwick, Cully, unidentified woman, Frederick von Stade, Mrs. George Mead, Electra Bostwick, Seymour Knox, Flora, Helen Hitchcock Clark, unidentified man, and (seated) Chi Bohlen and Whitney Tower.

"Dev." & Flora leading procession.

I would imagine that, at one point in time, everybody wanted to be in Show-Biz. I know I did.

Thanks to Aunt Foofie [Flora], my big chance arrived in the middle 1930s, when the film *Top Hat* with Fred Astaire and Ginger Rogers was released. Whitney Tower saw this movie something like sixteen times, and as a result, Aunt Foofie was convinced that he should take tap dancing lessons. In fact, she thought it would be wonderful for *all* of us to take lessons!

Our teacher was a little old lady from Augusta, Georgia, who knew *one* tap routine to the tune of "The Sidewalks of New York." We worked like dogs to learn all the steps, but it became very

evident after the fourth or fifth lesson that we all had two left feet . . . that is, except for Whit.

Aunt Foofie did not despair, however, and she formed the four of us into a musical act. I learned to play "The Sidewalks of New York" on the piano and my sister, Dolly, and Pam sang the lyrics, while Whit performed the tap routine which by now he had learned to perfection. Our leader booked us into a number of cocktail parties, where we would arrive in our limousine, with Nelson Mead at the wheel of a yellow Model-A, four-door convertible.

At first we were a smashing success, but as time went on, namely, the second week, we discovered that the same audience was at the same cocktail parties and that the time had come when they had had their bellyfull of "The Sidewalks of New York"!

(For a while thereafter, all the invitations Cully and Aunt Foofie received had a written addendum which said: "This invitation is null and void if Flora shows up with another one of her damn Dog and Pony Acts.")

As a result of all this and with no outlet to perform our great act, we decided to disband and go our separate ways (primarily to boarding school . . . a great relief to Cully).

Thus the end of my Show-Biz career!

In closing, however, I might point out that if you don't believe any of the above, I suggest you go to the Belmont Racetrack in June . . . and as the horses approach the track and the band starts playing "The Sidewalks of New York," direct your field glasses to the Press Box. I'm positive you'll see an old sportswriter doing a tap routine for the benefit of his fellow journalists! . . . a routine, I might add, that would never have been born if it had not been for the foresight and perseverance of our marvelous Aunt Foofie!!!

Frederick H. von Stade

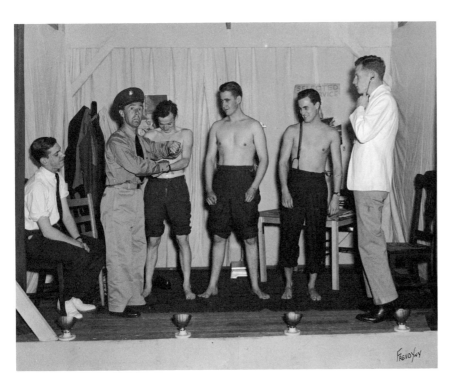

Amateur theatrical, "The Induction." Players are (from left): Whitney Tower, Seymour Knox, Nelson Mead, Thomas Clark, Toby Hilliard, and Frederick von Stade.

Top left: Flora salmon fishing in the York River, Canada, 1940.

Lower left: Flora playing croquet at Hobe Sound with Lady Margaret (Mrs. John) Walker and Averell Harriman, 1975.

Center right: Flora at a costume party hosted by the Payson family, with her cousin Joan Whitney (Mrs. Charles Shipman) Payson (center) and her daughter Pamela. Joan Whitney Payson was a Trustee of the Metropolitan Museum of Art from 1960 until her death in 1975, donor of the Joan Whitney Payson Galleries at the Metropolitan Museum, and, at the time of this photograph, owner of the New York Mets baseball team.

Having known Flora for over fifty years, I feel I appreciated her wonderful qualities better than most people. Her only failure I know was when Frances and I were staying with Cully and her in Paris for the "Arc de Triomphe" horse race and the three of them tried to instill some culture into me, some appreciation of all the wonderful things they showed me. I came away with the greatest appreciation for the Folies Bergère!

I often think of the wonderful times we had playing croquet with her in Old Westbury, salmon fishing on the York River, and just visiting in Aiken, where she gave me lots of lilies of the valley to start a bed that still reminds me of her.

Another pleasant memory was taking her to the old Jamaica racetrack in a snowstorm, where she deputized for Sonny and accepted the Jockey Club Gold Cup which made "Counterpoint" the horse of the year in 1951.

Ivor G. Balding

Flora Whitney Miller was a childhood friend of my husband, Tommy, and best friend throughout their lives of my sister-in-law Helen Hitchcock Clark. They enjoyed each other's company, reminiscing of their wonderfully special childhood together. When I married into the Hitchcock family, she included me and I remember many happy times together.

Margaret Mellon Hitchcock

Above: G. Macculloch Miller, *Lilies of the Valley,* 1964, watercolor on paper.

Facing page: Flora and Margaret Mellon (Mrs. Thomas) Hitchcock in Aiken in the 1930s.

Seymour H. Knox, recognized as one of the most knowledgeable and dedicated patrons of American art in the twentieth century, was a lifelong friend of Flora and one of the few people in Aiken, where both had family homes, who shared her interest in art and museums. For over sixty years, Seymour Knox has been the guiding force of the Albright-Knox Art Gallery in Buffalo. The Albright Art Gallery became the Albright-Knox Art Gallery in 1962 in honor of his patronage, and he is now Honorary Chairman of its governing authority, the Buffalo Fine Arts Academy.

Frederick H. von Stade retired in 1984 as Senior Vice President of the Taft Broadcasting Company, where he had worked for over thirty years. The von Stades lived across the street from Flora's family in Aiken. Mrs. von Stade joined Flora and Mrs. George Mead in establishing the Aiken Day School in the squash court on Flora's property.

Ivor G. Balding came to the United States in 1936 from England as a polo player and worked for Cornelius Vanderbilt (Sonny) Whitney. After attending Cornell University, he became head of the Whitney farm in Old Westbury, and has been a friend of members of the Whitney family for the past fifty years.

Margaret Mellon Hitchcock, daughter of Mary Hill Taylor and William Larimer Mellon, is the widow of Thomas Hitchcock. Her husband's sister, the late Helen Hitchcock Clark, was one of Flora's closest friends. Margaret Mellon Hitchcock was Flora's neighbor in Aiken, Old Westbury, and at 10 Gracie Square.

Banshee and Banco

Whitney Tower

Above:
Photograph from the
*Long Island Sunday
Press*, January 22, 1956,
showing Flora with her
poodle Banco and her
long-haired dachshund
Banshee at home.

Left:
G. Macculloch Miller,
Banco, 1960, oil on
canvas. Inscribed "Banco,
GMM, Paris, 1960."

Dogs, particularly poodles and long-haired dachshunds, played an important part in Ma's life. She didn't want to trot them around the ring at the Westminster or anything like that. Far from it. She just wanted them around most of the time, and it mattered not one tiny bit to her if some of us who were also around most of the time failed to recognize the same lovable qualities she so admired in her friends. The two pictured here with her in Old Westbury in 1956 are Banshee and Banco. Before Banshee there was a dachshund named Hexi who, when she wasn't being programmed to nip at every passing heel, found time to produce offspring with names like Bodo and Solo, the latter so named because he arrived in a litter of one and with a conformation which included a hideous undercut shark jaw. Bodo became Pam's, while I—no doubt because of all the endearing remarks I had made about Hexi—was given custody of Solo. I couldn't give the bum away.

Banco was Ma's last great canine pride and joy. He became something of a celebrity. For example, none of the family's station wagons came equipped with radios because, "Darling, you know that radio noises upset Banco so." Cully's visits to the Ritz Bar in Paris had to be rescheduled if Scott was using the car to chauffeur Banco to his hairdresser. The highlight of Banco's career and, for that matter, a landmark in the history of the United States Lines, occurred in 1952. On the voyage from France to New York, Ma was noticeably disturbed by Banco's kennel accommodations topside on the spanking new superliner the *S.S. United States*. This definitely called for action, and who better to lodge a protest with than fellow traveler and close friend Vincent Astor, the most influential big wheel in the U.S. Lines board room. The results were startling but not entirely unexpected: before her next sailing, the *United States* was equipped with new, enlarged kennels. I always thought they should have had a plaque saying, "Courtesy of Banco Miller."

Whitney Tower; biographical note, p. 46.

A Sporting Lady

John LeBoutillier

"Come on, Keith. Oh, Keith Keith, let's get going." The shouts were coming from the living room as I entered the house. It was September 1985. The Mets were playing at night in St. Louis. The previous two nights, the Mets had defeated the Cardinals to come within three games in the pennant race. Now, if they could only win tonight, they would have a real chance to win the pennant.

My grandmother sat in her accustomed seat on the sofa, one hand gripping a cigarette holder, the other nervously pulling on her lower lip as first baseman Keith Hernandez took his place in the batter's box.

"Keith Keith," as she referred to Hernandez, was one of her favorites. She also was crazy about Mookie Wilson, Gary Carter, and Darryl Strawberry. Her nurses kidded her that Keith was her secret "boyfriend." She would always smile at the mention of his name.

Those baseball fans who watched games with her have all said what a shame it was that she died during this (1986) season, the Mets' greatest year. But anyone who watched the playoffs and World Series must have noticed repeated miracles: Lenny Dykstra's home run, Ray Knight's clutch hits, and that unbelievable "come-back from certain defeat" in game six. It crossed my mind over and over that my grandmother was up in heaven, secretly managing "her team" and making sure they would win, no matter what it took.

When the Mets were paraded down Broadway after winning the World Series, I wished my grandmother could have seen it with me on television. But, certainly she did see it. And knowing her loyalty and devotion to that team, she'll see to it that they keep winning from now on. And, as for "Keith Keith," she'll make sure he ends up in the Hall of Fame.

John LeBoutillier, son of Pamela Tower and Thomas LeBoutillier, was a member of the United States Congress from the State of New York from 1980 to 1982. He has dedicated his life to obtaining the release of prisoners of war taken during the Vietnam War who are still imprisoned in Southeast Asia.

Flora, with "tennis racket" cane given to her by her son Leverett, and her grandson John LeBoutillier in Old Westbury, 1979.

G.M.M.   F.W.M.   SONNY W.

HAVANA - 1931 - RACE COURSE

Facing page: Album page with photographs of Flora with her "big catch," a shark caught from her father's yacht, c. 1920 (top left); Harry Payne Whitney's yacht, *Whileaway*, c. 1920 (top right); and Flora, Cully, and her brother Cornelius Vanderbilt (Sonny) Whitney at the races in Havana, 1931 (bottom). Sonny wears a black armband, mourning the death of his and Flora's father, Harry Payne Whitney, in 1930.

Top right: Flora teaching her daughter Flora to cast as her son Leverett watches, Newport, 1938.

Center right: Flora enjoying being towed in her canoe on Forked Lake in the Adirondacks, 1932.

Bottom right: Flora in shooting competition at Aiken, 1940.

Below, left: "Duck Soup" hunting camp near Charleston, South Carolina, seen through Spanish moss, 1945. Most of Flora's homes throughout her life had been previously established by her family. One of the places she and her husband, Cully, created for themselves and enjoyed the most was this modest house, designed by Cully. It was used as the headquarters for many duck shoots with family and friends.

Bottom left: Flora duck shooting at dawn near "Duck Soup," 1945.

Leader of the Whitney Museum of American Art

Lloyd Goodrich
Philip Johnson
Sandra Payson

Photograph of Flora in front of the new Whitney Museum at 22 West Fifty-fourth Street, from the "For and About Women" section of the *Long Island Sunday Press*, January 22, 1956, accompanying an article entitled, "Museum's Lady Skipper," which recognized Flora as "an extraordinary woman who has managed to raise four children . . . and a new museum building. The daughter of the late Gertrude Vanderbilt Whitney, the sculptor and art philanthropist, she is president of the Whitney Museum of American Art, the nation's leading showcase of U.S. painting and sculpture."

To us on the staff of the Whitney Museum, Flora Whitney Miller was a dedicated fellow worker in the great cause of American art. In the twenty-four years of her presidency the Museum went through the most crucial stages of its growth. It grew from a pioneer institution with no support outside of the Whitney family to a museum with broad-based support from an enlarged Board of Trustees and from the new Friends of the Museum. From its birthplace, four re-modeled old houses on Eighth Street, it expanded first to a modern building on Fifty-Fourth Street, and in 1966 to its present home, one of the most innovative and gen-uinely functional museum buildings in the country. And there were fundamental changes in aims and activities. Our original ambition to build a historic collection of American art, past and present, in competi-tion with older New York museums, was superseded by concentration on the art of our century, combined with an active program of exhibitions of American art of the past. Our early abstention from one-man shows of living artists was succeeded by major retro-spectives of leading artists of our time. Schol-arship in the then-neglected American field was encouraged and sponsored. Publications expanded from the modest exhibition cata-logues of the 1940s to the most extensive publishing program on American art. In that quarter-century of Mrs. Miller's presidency, the Whitney Museum came of full age.

Throughout all these changes, for us of the Museum staff Flora Whitney Miller was not an aloof authority but our friend—warm-hearted, understanding, responsive, and with a delightful sense of humor. It was always a pleasure to meet with her and to share our problems and successes. In our relations with her and with Cully Miller there was no trace of officialism; we were companions in the same cause, the well-being and growth of living American art, and of the Museum we all loved.

Lloyd Goodrich

Flora Miller was a Great Lady to me in my youth. Her mere presence would encourage me in the arts in a way no lesser person's could have.

The continuity she gave to the idea of American art gave us all hope in our—sometimes discouraged—efforts to keep going.

My most vivid memory of her was a grand entrance she once made to a meeting in the Museum of Modern Art, not merely as a representative of one or two institutions but as a living embodiment of the great flow of *American Art* itself.

Philip Johnson

My maternal cousin Flora Miller was a charming, gracious, intelligent lady, who was President of the Whitney Museum for many years.

When I was elected a Board member in 1975, I was feeling somewhat uncertain and green, as I had never been a part of a board membership and, having just returned from ten years in Europe, needed a bit of guidance.

Mrs. Miller, in her understated manner, knew how to guide the ship with a steady hand and how to deal in a personal and decisive way at the Board meetings. I for one felt welcome and was made to feel at ease.

Her daughter, Flora Miller Biddle, in her years as President of the Museum, exhibited the same quiet, intense and personal approach.

Sandra Payson

Lloyd Goodrich began his sixty-year association with Gertrude Vanderbilt Whitney and the Whitney Museum of American Art in 1924 as a writer for The Arts, *a publication supported by Gertrude Vanderbilt Whitney. He joined the staff of the new Whitney Museum in 1930 as a researcher and writer, and was Associate Director from 1948 to 1958 and Director from 1958 to 1968. He is now an Honorary Trustee. He is recognized as the leading authority on the work of Albert Pinkham Ryder, Thomas Eakins, Winslow Homer, and Edward Hopper. In 1979 he received the award for Distinguished Service to the Arts from the American Academy and Institute of Arts and Letters.*

Philip Johnson, architect, has been a Trustee of the Museum of Modern Art since 1957. He served as a member of the Planning Committee of the Whitney Museum of American Art (1974–75) and contributed to the report of the Committee which has guided the leadership of the Whitney Museum to the present time.

Sandra Payson; biographical note, p. 27.

The Three Museum Agreement

Blanchette H. Rockefeller

Those of us dedicated to the well-being of the museums of New York City will always remember Flora Whitney Miller. I recall with admiration her vision concerning the vital role cultural institutions play in our city and the tireless energy she expended for the Whitney. I particularly remember her sensitivity, tact, and dignity at the time we were crafting the Three Museum Agreement symbolized in this photograph.

Blanchette H. Rockefeller

© Arnold Newman

Above: Flora, President of the Whitney Museum of American Art, seated with Roland L. Redmond, President of the Metropolitan Museum of Art (left) and her cousin John Hay (Jock) Whitney, President of the Museum of Modern Art, in a photograph documenting the Three Museum Agreement signed in September 1947. Each president is shown with works of art associated with his or her institution.

Facing page, top: Flora and Blanchette H. Rockefeller (Mrs. John D. Rockefeller 3rd) at the opening of the Whitney Museum of American Art at Madison Avenue and Seventy-fifth Street, September 27, 1966. The photograph appeared in *Vogue,* November 15, 1966.

In 1947, the Whitney Museum of American Art, the Metropolitan Museum of Art, and the Museum of Modern Art signed what was known as the Three Museum Agreement, intended to further collaboration between the three institutions. In his 1970 history of the Metropolitan, Calvin Tomkins described the collaboration:

"Each museum recognized the others' primary interest in a certain area—the Metropolitan's in 'classic art,' the Museum of Modern Art's in European and American visual art of the present and recent past, the Whitney's in American art. In the interests of 'rendering better service to the public and effecting economies,' the Metropolitan would refrain from active buying of modern art. All three museums would lend freely to one another for exhibitions and for educational purposes. The coalition between the Whitney and the Metropolitan was confirmed. Furthermore, the Metropolitan agreed to 'deposit with the Modern Museum such paintings, drawings, prints and sculpture . . . as it believes can be more appropriately exhibited at the Modern Museum,' while the Modern Museum agreed to sell to the Metropolitan, for the sum of $191,000 payable in four annual installments, a total of forty works of art that both museums had decided would be better off there. . . . They include two Cézannes, three Matisse oils, two Rouaults, three Seurat drawings, five Maillol sculptures, and two very fine Picassos—*Woman in White*, and *La Coiffure*.

A *ménage à trois*, as the French never tire of informing us, is often stimulating but rarely peaceful. In no time at all the Three Museum Agreement began showing signs of strain. [Alfred] Barr was said to be resentful over the loss of *Woman in White*. The Whitney Museum architects were squabbling with the Metropolitan architects over plans for the Whitney wing. The Metropolitan's rejection of several pictures recommended [for acquisition] that year by Juliana Force led to her angry withdrawal in 1948 as their adviser on American art. . . . In the hope of resolving their various differences and clearing the air, Roland Redmond invited the key staff members of all three museums to dinner at the Brook Club, where in the most genteel surroundings the *ménage* rather noisily came apart. . . .

[Lloyd] Goodrich and [Hermon] More decided . . . that there was no compelling reason to merge with an institution that was so hostile to their point of view. Juliana Force agreed—she was still in the hospital at the time, undergoing treatment for the cancer that would kill her a few months later. The Whitney trustees reached the same conclusion not long afterward. The advantages of the coalition, they decided, were not worth the loss of their museum's individual identity. They abandoned all plans to build on property adjoining the Metropolitan, and on September 30, 1948—just one year after the signing—the Whitney formally withdrew from the Three Museum Agreement."

Calvin Tomkins
Excerpt from *Merchants and Masterpieces:
The Story of the Metropolitan Museum of Art*
(E.P. Dutton & Co., Inc., 1970), pp. 306–09

Private to Public

David M. Solinger

David M. Solinger is senior partner of the law firm Solinger Grosz & Goldwasser and has been a Trustee of the Whitney Museum of American Art since 1961. He has served as President of the Museum (1966–74) and Chairman of the Board (1974–77), and is currently Honorary President. He was also a founder and the first President of the Friends of the Whitney Museum of American Art (1956–59) and chaired the fund-raising drive for the building and endowment of the Whitney Museum on Madison Avenue and Seventy-fifth Street. Together with Flora, he built the Friends as a patronage base for the Museum, and is greatly responsible for its successful transition from private to public institution.

This photograph records what surely is one of the most significant milestones in the history of the Whitney Museum of American Art.

When Flora Miller's mother, Gertrude Vanderbilt Whitney, founded the Museum in 1930 she contributed substantial capital funds, the income from which, even twenty-five years later, continued to pay for its day-to-day operating expenses. But with the coming of age of the American artist and the escalating prices commanded by his work, the Museum's purchase funds became more and more inadequate and the Friends of the Whitney Museum was organized in 1956 to supplement these funds and nourish the Permanent Collection.

Was membership in the Friends to be the first step in a continuing process of involving non-family members in the affairs of the Museum? Or was it to remain a small, family museum? The Museum's future depended upon the answer to these questions by Flora, who was President of the Museum's Board of Trustees.

On a lovely spring day in 1958, over lunch at the stately old Ambassador Hotel on Fifty-first Street and Park Avenue, I suggested to Flora that in the face of increasing inflation, what started as the philanthropy of her mother would soon transcend the ability of any single person or family to support. She readily agreed; but she was deeply troubled by the prospect of "going public." Her mother had been a private patron and Flora regarded herself as the legatee of a sacred trust which she felt obliged to perpetuate. She had difficulty reconciling what she perceived as her duty to her mother with public support and governance. This photo shows how she reconciled the seeming conflict; and the history of the Museum in the last quarter-century is evidence of the public-spiritedness and wisdom of her decision.

Flora, President of the Whitney Museum of
American Art, with the first group of non-family
Trustees elected to the Board on July 1, 1961. From
left: David M. Solinger, B. H. Friedman, John I. H.
Baur, Flora, Roy R. Neuberger, Lloyd Goodrich,
Arthur G. Altschul, Michael H. Irving.

Debt to the Past

Roy R. Neuberger
James A. Michener

Helen Appleton Read speaking at the luncheon held at the Hotel Plaza on December 14, 1964 to celebrate the 50th Anniversary, to the day, of the opening of the Whitney Studio, which marked the beginning of a series of activities that led eventually to the founding of the Whitney Museum of American Art. Helen Appleton Read's early interest in the work and patronage of Gertrude Vanderbilt Whitney, her friendship with Juliana Force, Director of the Whitney Museum (1930–48), and her professional and social association with Whitney Studio Club artists as a writer and critic made her an engaging speaker at the 50th Anniversary luncheon. Others on the dais are (from left): Flora, Roy R. Neuberger, James A. Michener, Mrs. H. Gates Lloyd, Cornelius Vanderbilt (Sonny) Whitney, and Flora's cousin Gladys (Vanderbilt), the Countess Laszlo Széchényi. In addition to those shown in the photograph, others who paid tribute to Gertrude Vanderbilt Whitney on this occasion were Henry Schnakenberg, Edward Steichen, and Lloyd Goodrich.

I quite vividly recall the luncheon at the elegant Persian Room of the Plaza Hotel held on December 14, 1964. I remember how pleased I was when Flora Miller and others asked me to be the master of ceremonies for that memorable occasion.

The Whitney Studio, which was opened by Flora's mother, Gertrude Vanderbilt Whitney, played a very important role in promoting works of art by American artists, and its influence was widely felt in the art world.

This luncheon, which celebrated the 50th Anniversary of the opening of the Whitney Studio, subtly focused on the raising of funds for the Whitney Museum. The desire was to obtain support from the many relatives of the Whitney family who up to that time were quite far removed from the Whitney Museum and the American art world.

I remember being impressed by the particularly inspiring speech given by Helen Appleton Read—a wonderful person whose sister worked for the Whitney Museum for a number of years. I also recall James A. Michener (the writer of a multitude of books) telling of his many visits to the Whitney Museum on Eighth Street, and how these visits stirred his budding interest in the art world. He began buying works of art, and since that early beginning he has amassed a considerable collection of art.

Roy R. Neuberger

As a young man working in New York I frequently stopped by the gallery on Eighth Street to see what new canvases were on display, and it was there principally that I gained my understanding of American art. How vividly those memories survive. The Whitney performed a valiant service in those days, and I was pleased when it moved uptown to larger quarters.

There also I pursued my education and without the Museum's cicerone quality I might never have become interested in collecting on my own. So my debt to the Whitney is considerable, especially to its fine series of publications. It was in that frame of mind that I attended the luncheon shown in the photograph.

Thank you for the years of companionship.

James A. Michener

Roy R. Neuberger is an investment banker and senior partner of Neuberger & Berman, and was a Trustee of the Whitney Museum of American Art (1961–69). During the campaign to raise funds to build the new Whitney Museum at Madison Avenue and Seventy-fifth Street, he served as Chairman of the Finance Committee and organized an auction for the benefit of the campaign that realized five percent of the total campaign goal. In 1968 his gift of a large part of his collection of American painting and sculpture to the State of New York created the Neuberger Museum at the State University of New York at Purchase. Designed by Philip Johnson, it opened in 1974.

James A. Michener, Pulitzer prize-winning author, established a collection of twentieth-century American art which toured extensively in the 1960s. The James A. Michener Collection was given to the University of Texas at Austin in 1970.

A New Building

Michael Graves

The Whitney Museum of American Art announced today (Monday, June 17, 1963) that it had contracted to sell its present building at 22 West Fifty-fourth Street to the Museum of Modern Art and that it would erect a new one, approximately three times as large, on a site at the southeast corner of Madison Avenue and East Seventy-fifth Street. Marcel Breuer, the noted architect, will be retained to design the new museum, which will be his first work to be erected in Manhattan. Michael H. Irving will be the consulting architect.

Mrs. G. Macculloch Miller, President of the Whitney, called the decision a "milestone" in the history of the thirty-three-year-old Museum. She said the Museum's Trustees decided on the move because of a pressing need for more space in which to show the present collection and to maintain an active schedule of loan exhibitions. The Museum has the largest and most comprehensive collection of twentieth-century American art of any public institution in the country.

The new site has a Madison Avenue frontage of 103 feet 8 inches and 125 feet on Seventy-fifth Street, making a total area of almost 13,000 square feet. This is almost twice the size of the approximately 6,800 square foot plot on which the present Museum stands.

Mrs. Miller said the Museum will continue to occupy its present building until the new one is completed approximately three years from now. A major fund-raising drive will be launched in the near future to raise money for the new building and for an endowment to carry on an expanded schedule of activities.

She said a series of galleries will be set aside in the new museum for the continuous exhibition of art from the Permanent Collection, while other rooms will be devoted to loan exhibitions such as the Museum's Annuals, its one-man shows, and its surveys of different trends and movements. At present, many of the Museum's loan exhibitions fill the entire building with the result that the Permanent Collection spends much of its time in storage or on loan elsewhere.

The new property will be purchased from the Jonathan Woodner Company. Ian Woodner, President, had planned a cooperative apartment on the site, and was persuaded to abandon this because of the Whitney's interest in the property and his own great interest in art.

Internationally recognized as one of the great innovators of modern architecture, Marcel Breuer's career began in Germany at the Bauhaus, with which he was connected during 1920–28. After practicing in Berlin and then London, he was invited in 1937 to come to Harvard by Walter Gropius, under whom he had studied at the Bauhaus. As a partner of Gropius, Breuer made significant contributions in the application of Bauhaus principles to American housing. In recent years, Breuer has been increasingly concerned with large-scale public structures, both here and abroad, the most notable being the UNESCO headquarters in Paris (1958). Others include the New Dormitory residence and community halls and the laboratory wing and lecture hall of the Technology Building on the campus of New York University in the Bronx (1961).

Excerpt from the
Whitney Museum of American Art
press release, June 17, 1963

Flora, President of the Whitney Museum of American Art, with Marcel Breuer (second from right), architect of the Whitney Museum at Madison Avenue and Seventy-fifth Street, Lloyd Goodrich, Director of the Museum, and her daughter Flora, Vice President of the Museum, on the occasion of the announcement of the plans for the new building, December 11, 1963.

In the designing of the project and after establishing its workings and its program, we have faced the first and most important problem: what should a museum look like, a museum in Manhattan? Surely it should work, it should fulfill its requirements. But what is its relationship to the New York landscape? What does it express? What is its architectural message?

It is easier to say first what it should *not* look like. It should not look like a business or office building, nor should it look like a place of light entertainment. Its form and its material should have identity and weight in the neighborhood of 50-story skyscrapers, of mile-long bridges, in the midst of the dynamic jungle of our colorful city. It should be an independent and self-reliant unit, exposed to history, and at the same time it should have a visual connection to the street. It should transform the vitality of the street into the sincerity and profundity of art. . . .

To emphasize the completeness of the architectural form, the granite façades on both streets are separated from the neighboring fronts: an attempt to solve the inherent problem of a corner building, which otherwise could easily look like a quarter-section of something. The project transforms the building into a unit, an element, a nucleus, and lends it a direction towards Madison Avenue. The overall granite facing, homogeneous, extending out and over towards Madison Avenue, reaching down into the sunken garden with openings which grow out of the surface, with the modulation of the Madison Avenue gap between it and the neighboring buildings, with the granite parapet along the sidewalk and with the structural concrete form of the bridge—all this is an attempt to form the building itself as a sculpture. However, it is a sculpture with rather serious functional requirements.

Marcel Breuer
Excerpt from "The Architect's Approach to the Design of the Whitney Museum," *The Whitney Review*, 1965–66.

Ezra Stoller © ESTO

Façade of the Whitney Museum of American Art on West Eighth Street, designed by G. Macculloch Miller's architectural firm, Noel and Miller, and incorporating four pre-existing buildings (including Gertrude Vanderbilt Whitney's studio) at 8, 10, 12 and 14 West Eighth Street. This was the Museum's home from its founding in 1930 until 1954.

Façade of the Whitney Museum of American Art, 22 West Fifty-fourth Street, designed by Noel and Miller. This property was generously given to the Whitney Museum by the Trustees of the Museum of Modern Art and was the home of the Whitney Museum from 1954 until 1966. The Museum of Modern Art bought the property back from the Whitney Museum for approximately $2 million.

Though I met Mrs. Miller only once, for a brief afternoon visit just a few weeks before she died, she was so charming on that occasion that I didn't want the day to end. It is no wonder that the Whitney Museum was in such vigorous health during her time, for she was a woman with extraordinary spirit and heart. Clearly, she was special.

She received my description of the expanded Whitney Museum of American Art with great perception, and our conversation following my presentation revealed the visual depth of her understanding. That conversation, and her endorsement of what I was doing, enriched my experience of designing this building for the institution that had been such a large part of her life.

Michael Graves

Michael Graves, architect, is Schirmer Professor of Architecture at Princeton University, where he has taught since 1962. He is best known for the Portland Building in Portland, Oregon, the Humana Corporate Headquarters Building in Louisville, Kentucky, and the Public Library in San Juan Capistrano, California. In 1981 he was selected by the Trustees of the Whitney Museum of American Art to design the expanded Whitney Museum. The design for the building shown here was announced on March 10, 1987.

The Whitney Museum of American Art, 945 Madison Avenue at Seventy-fifth Street, designed by Marcel Breuer.

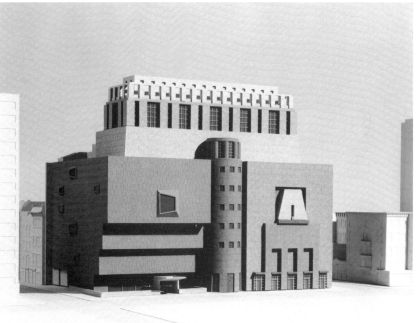

Michael Graves, *Model for the Proposed Expanded Whitney Museum of American Art.*

Cornerstone of a Dream

The following is the address delivered by Flora at the cornerstone ceremonies initiating the construction of the new Whitney Museum of American Art, Madison Avenue at Seventy-fifth Street, October 20, 1964:

"I cannot tell you how gratified I am to see so many of our old friends and new neighbors here today.

It has seemed to us appropriate to place certain documents in our cornerstone, which will later be incorporated in our new building. These include:

Memorabilia relating to the founding of the Museum

Various accounts of its growth and its collections

A catalogue of our current Edward Hopper exhibition

A catalogue—which means much to me personally—of the 1943 memorial exhibition of my mother's work at the old Whitney Museum on Eighth Street

I now place these in the stone, with faith in the future and deep gratitude in my heart to everyone here for helping us to celebrate this crucial moment in the birth of the new Whitney Museum."

Facing page: Flora setting the cornerstone at the ceremonies on October 20, 1964, marking the beginning of the construction of the new Whitney Museum of American Art at Madison Avenue and Seventy-fifth Street. Next to Flora are (from left): Lloyd Goodrich, Director of the Whitney Museum, August Heckscher, Director of the Twentieth Century Fund, and Mayor Robert F. Wagner.

Below: Flora at the eastern edge of the construction site of the new Whitney Museum, October 20, 1964.

ARCHITECT
MARCEL BREUER & ASSOCIATES
NEW YORK, N. Y.

CONSULTING AR
MICHA
NEW

STRUCTURA
PAUL W
NE

The New Whitney Museum

William A. Marsteller
Jacqueline Kennedy Onassis

The following remarks were delivered by Flora prior to cutting the ribbon at the dedication ceremonies for the new Whitney Museum of American Art at Madison Avenue and Seventy-fifth Street on September 27, 1966:

"Three years ago our Board of Trustees had the courage (and it took courage) to embark on a radical expansion of the Whitney Museum and its activities on behalf of American art. Two years ago we stood near this same spot and laid the cornerstone of the beautiful building which Marcel Breuer had designed for us. Today that building stands before us, outshining any of our expectations. We enter, not without awe, a new chapter in our history.

I cannot tell you what this moment means to me. It is the culmination of a dream that my mother had nearly sixty years ago. As I cut this ribbon my heart is full of gratitude to the devoted people, our Trustees, our staff and others, who helped with such generosity to give that dream, that vision, reality. It seems a fitting moment to dedicate this building, and at the same time to rededicate ourselves, to the ideal which the Whitney has always stood for—the service of this country's living art."

Cutting the ribbon to officially open the new Whitney Museum must have been one of the most satisfying days in Flora Miller's illustrious life.

A dream had become a reality. The days and nights of planning, the thousands of hours of meeting with architects, engineers, city officials, museum experts, fund-raisers, and, most of all, prospective donors, had been rewarded with praise for this new home of what was rapidly becoming one of New York's most important cultural institutions.

Flora Whitney Miller had long been committed to broadening the management of the Museum so that it would not be so dependent upon future generations of the Whitney family to provide the direction and funding for continued survival and growth. At the same time, throughout her life, she kept the Whitney dedication to the character of the Museum steady. She was modest, patient and quietly persistent, and resisted all attempts to steer the Museum away from its basic reason for being.

In many ways the opening of the new Museum marked the affirmation of its role as a national, not simply New York, institution. The group surrounding Flora at this ribbon-cutting ceremony attests to that, for it includes American art collectors from across the nation. Immediately after this ceremony, a new National Committee, chaired by Jacqueline Kennedy, held its first meeting and declared, among other things, that the Whitney Museum should truly be the preeminent home of American art.

This picture, it seems to me, speaks to this. Flora—her arms open wide—seems to be welcoming everyone to this unique national cultural treasure.

William A. Marsteller

Facing page: Flora at the joyous moment of cutting the ribbon at the dedication of the new Whitney Museum, September 27, 1966, with (from left): Jacqueline Kennedy, William A. Marsteller, Nathan Cummings, Flora, Robert W. Sarnoff, Marylou (Mrs. Cornelius Vanderbilt) Whitney, and Lloyd Goodrich.

It had long been a dream and on this beautiful autumn day with Mrs. Miller we saw it come true.

Jacqueline Kennedy Onassis

Flora, President of the Whitney Museum of American Art, at the first meeting of the 1965 National Committee, chaired by Jacqueline Kennedy, in the Trustees Room of the new Whitney Museum, September 27, 1966. From left are: John I.H. Baur, Associate Director, Flora, Jacqueline Kennedy, Lloyd Goodrich, Director, and Flora Biddle, Vice President.

The following remarks were delivered by Flora to the Trustees at their first meeting in the new Whitney Museum on June 7, 1966:

"This is an exciting moment! Our new building is beautiful beyond words. I doubt that it will ever seem more so to me than now . . . when all of you who made it possible are meeting here for the first time.

It seems such a short time ago, doesn't it, when we first met together as Trustees? We knew we were there to plan and build something new . . . something, I feel, totally consistent with my mother's ideals on behalf of the American artist.

This Board's first important decision was to build our *own* museum—away from the shadow of any existing institution. Not long after that decision, I remember when David [Solinger], heading a Planning Committee, told us we would have to raise $8 million to accomplish this . . . and even more amazing, saying that *we could*! This seems like yesterday . . . in spite of the fact that a year ago I wondered if the time would ever come when we weren't *completely* preoccupied with fundraising. I think that time has come. Not that our campaign is completed . . . there is still much to be done. Not that ever again will there be a time when this Board is not searching for new sources of support. But that *now* we can balance our awareness of *this* against the responsibility entrusted to each of us to assure that this Museum plays an expanding and vital role, because I think all of you, as you feel joy at the beauty of this building, also feel the seriousness and depth of the challenge it imposes on us.

You are marvelously dedicated Trustees . . . you have been unbelievably generous with your time and money. Again and again your talents, creative and organizational, have been indispensable to our progress. Truly this is your Museum. It is the product of your vision and your hard work.

I particularly want to thank our devoted staff for their imaginative and unremitting labors during the past hectic period. If I now single out a few of you to mention, it does not mean that I am not aware and grateful for the work of everyone else. I do particularly want to thank those of you who have assumed committee chairmanships: David Solinger, head of the Planning Committee, for his far-sighted leadership of the campaign as a whole. Benno Schmidt, as head of the Major Gifts Committee, for being directly responsible for a number of our most important gifts. Alan Temple, for his unstinting efforts on the financial side of the campaign. Bob Friedman, of the Building Committee, for so many hours of skilled, intelligent overseeing of the planning and construction of this building from its inception. And Michael Irving for the time and professional assistance he has freely given. And to Roy Neuberger, Chairman of the Finance Committee, for so many things besides organizing an auction which brought in a vital five percent of our total goal. And to Jack Baur's constant and untiring . . . maybe I mean *tiring*, efforts over prospective donors . . . showing them the building, explaining our objectives and our ambitions, and writing the English language in a literate and sophisticated manner. And Lloyd Goodrich for taking over many of the things that had to be abandoned by other members of the staff. He will be trailing clouds of glory forever when our first show . . . *his* show opens in September.

I know all of us want to express our gratitude to Bowen and Gurin, and especially Ben Thompson, for doing such diligent, competent work on the campaign. Also for the first time in the Museum's history, thanks to Mr. [Leon] Levine, we have had professional guidance in our press and public relations. Mr. Levine's results speak for themselves, and we have learned a great deal from his association with us.

Before turning this meeting over to you, let me say how *proud* I am of this Board. I want to thank each of you for being the kind of devoted trustees museum presidents dream about . . . but never really expect to meet.

The new Whitney Museum is capable of greatness. Because *you* who have been entrusted with its ideals . . . and now its beautiful new home . . . *you* are capable of greatness. Four years of our association on this Board have convincingly demonstrated this. I hope charting the development of our Museum in the years ahead will be exhilarating for you. I'm sure it will be more fun than just raising money . . . and every bit as important.

Thank you all so much."

William A. Marsteller is founder of the advertising firm Marsteller, Inc. He was a Trustee of the Whitney Museum of American Art (1975–84) and a founding member of its 1965 National Committee. As a Trustee, he initiated innovative programs that helped the membership of the Museum become a major source of support for operations.

Jacqueline Kennedy Onassis, widow of the 35th President of the United States and of Aristotle Onassis, is an editor at Doubleday & Co. She was a Trustee of the Whitney Museum of American Art (1962–68) and Chairman of the 1965 National Committee, which had its first and only meeting at the time of the opening of the new Museum.

Artists

John I. H. Baur

Installation of works donated to the Whitney Museum of American Art in honor of the accomplishments of John I.H. Baur as Director of the Whitney Museum on the occasion of a surprise tribute dinner hosted by the Friends on June 5, 1974. The largest work in the photograph is *Goldenrod in December* by Charles Burchfield, purchased by Flora following her introduction to Burchfield by Jack Baur, and subsequently given to the Museum in his honor.

My first meeting with Flora Miller—at a Whitney Museum opening in the old Eighth Street building—was not auspicious. I had just been made curator and was feeling quite grand. In the opening hubbub I was talking to the sculptor William Zorach, and failed to hear the name of an effervescent lady who interrupted us to congratulate me on my new job. I shrugged her off, quite abruptly I'm afraid, then asked Bill who she was. When he stopped laughing he told me.

That Flora forgave me was a mark of her usual generosity. She had the great gift of putting people at their ease—even artists who must often have tested her patience with their varied quirks. I discovered this when I organized my first exhibition at the Whitney, surveying the work of Loren MacIver. In those distant days of 1953, the young MacIver was so shy she had to be bullied into coming to her own opening, but I think she was glad when Flora not only spoke warmly of her work but bought a painting from the exhibition.

One could multiply examples of Flora's genuine concern for artists. Bernard Reder—a very great sculptor and a very difficult man—was devoted to her. Her kindness tamed Philip Evergood's distrust of the rich and dispelled Charles Burchfield's social inarticulateness. After the latter's one-man show at the Whitney in 1956, Flora took his whole family back to 10 Gracie Square for a champagne dinner and bought his *Goldenrod in December*. Her spirit played a crucial part in establishing and nourishing the Whitney's policy of supporting living artists. We all loved her.

John I.H. Baur joined the staff of the Whitney Museum of American Art as Curator in 1951, and served as Associate Director from 1958 to 1968, during which time he guided the construction of the new Whitney Museum designed by Marcel Breuer. He was Director of the Museum from 1968 to 1974 and is now an Honorary Trustee. Recognized as a leading scholar of American art, his books, which are primary references, include: Revolution and Tradition in American Art *(1951),* Bradley Walker Tomlin *(1957),* Joseph Stella *(1971),* Philip Evergood *(1975), and* The Inlander: Life and Work of Charles Burchfield *(1982).*

Left: Flora with Jack Baur and his wife, Louise, c. 1965.

Below: Flora and Isabel Bishop at Gertrude Vanderbilt Whitney's studio, May 18, 1980. The work of Isabel Bishop has been exhibited at the Whitney Museum since 1933; a major retrospective of her work was presented in 1975.

The following is a poem written by Flora about Jack Baur, Director of the Whitney Museum of American Art, and his two predecessors, Lloyd Goodrich and Hermon More:

Mr. Baur and Mrs. Miller
Were how we addressed each other
Those many years ago.
But openings on Eighth Street
With liquor plus heat
Kept one highly aglow.

So Jack and Flora we soon became,
And I thank the dear gods for that.
Through all the years that followed
No fights, bad words or crimes
Disturbed the friendly times;
Only in fun we wallowed.

And Hermon and Lloyd and Jack and I
Were minced together like pie.
But ah but those wonderful men
Were all married to wonderful WOMEN.

The following is the text of a letter written to Flora by Isabel Bishop on May 7, 1967:

I was thrilled to know that you took a drawing, from my exhibition! It was good of you to go in, in the first place. And then, that you liked something well enough to have it, gave me great nourishment, for the spirit!

I look forward to, sometime, seeing you.

> With affectionate greetings,
> Isabel

3 Washington Square, New York
February 26, 1950

Dear Mrs. Miller:

American artists must have the most sincere appreciation for the great opportunities your mother and you have given them in making their work known to the public.

For my own part I feel deeply as to the opportunity that you have given me to show my work in its entirety in the present exhibition.

You no doubt know that the Whitney Studio Club gave me my first exhibition back in 1919, and the Museum has shown my canvases and water-colors every year since. I owe much to the Whitney Museum for the recognition that has come to me.

I think Lloyd Goodrich and Hermon More have done a fine job in organizing and hanging the show. It was done with great care and thoroughness,

Most sincerely,
Edward Hopper

Top left: Flora with Edward Hopper in front of his painting *Early Sunday Morning* (1930) at the private reception on November 14, 1961 for *American Art of Our Century*, an exhibition accompanied by a catalogue written by Lloyd Goodrich and John I.H. Baur, which celebrated the thirtieth anniversary of the opening of the Whitney Museum on November 18, 1931. Hopper's association with the Whitney Museum began with his first one-artist exhibition at the Whitney Studio Club in 1920. Gertrude Vanderbilt Whitney bought *Early Sunday Morning* when she was establishing an outstanding group of works of art with which to open the new Whitney Museum to the public in 1931. When Hopper's wife died in 1968, she left his entire artistic estate of more than two thousand oils, watercolors, drawings, and prints to the Whitney Museum in recognition of Hopper's gratitude for Gertrude Vanderbilt Whitney's early encouragement and the Museum's continued support of his work. The works by Edward Hopper now in the Permanent Collection of the Whitney Museum cover the full span of his creative life and represent the most extensive public collection of works by a single American artist.

Lower left: Letter from Edward Hopper to Flora, dated February 26, 1950. Hopper's first exhibition, which he here dates "1919," actually took place in January 1920; the "present exhibition" to which he refers was the Hopper retrospective at the Whitney Museum of American Art, February 11–March 26, 1950.

Facing page: Flora surrounded by artists at the opening of the exhibition of the S.C. Johnson & Son, Inc. collection, *Art: USA*, March 23, 1965.

The opening of the exhibition of the Johnson collection—*Art: USA* at the Whitney Museum of American Art brought together a large number of America's leading artists. Twenty-eight of them are shown here in a group photograph taken March 23, 1965 at the preview. They are shown with Mr. and Mrs. H. F. Johnson, Mrs. Flora Whitney Miller, President, and Mr. Lloyd Goodrich, Director of the Whitney Museum, and Lee Nordness who assembled the collection. Those in the photograph are:

1. Richard Pousette-Dart	12. Jonah Kinigstein	23. Will Barnet
2. Edwin Dickinson	13. Karl Zerbe	24. Robert Gwathmey
3. George Tooker	14. Paul Burlin	25. Paul Jenkins
4. Herbert Katzman	15. Theodoros Stamos	26. Mrs. Flora Whitney Miller
5. John Heliker	16. Margo Hoff	27. Mrs. Vclav Vytlacil
6. Richard Lytle	17. Mrs. Jimmy Ernst	28. Lloyd Goodrich
7. James Kearns	18. Lee Nordness	29. Milton Resnick
8. Leon Goldin	19. Isabel Bishop	30. Bernard Perlin
9. Ralston Crawford	20. Mr. and Mrs. H. F. Johnson	31. Mrs. John Von Wicht
10. Samuel Adler	21.	32. I. Rice Pereira
11. Mrs. Walter Plate	22. Mrs. Paul Jenkins	33. Joseph Hirsch

Patrons

Howard Lipman

It was about twenty-five years ago that the family-owned Whitney Museum began to bring in non-family members both as trustees and as members of the newly established Friends. I think it was about 1961 that I was invited to head the acquisitions committee for that year. I had no previous formal relationship with the Museum. I had known Jack Baur, then Associate Director of the Whitney; we had had a cordial relationship for some years. I did not know the majority of the Friends or many of the Trustees—so I came to my first committee meeting with some trepidation. I was becoming enthusiastic about contemporary American sculpture, but could not know whether the staff or Trustees would have any enthusiasm for my interests.

So I carried with me to this first meeting, with concern, some photographs of Alexander Calder's new, large stabiles. Calder was well known at that time for his mobiles, but in 1961 his large stabiles had had just one small exhibition in New York. Sandy was fabricat-ing these in France, and I had secured the photos from the Galerie Maeght in Paris. I entered this meeting with no way of knowing what to expect. We sat down, I think eight of us, Flora Miller at one end of the table, Jack Baur at the other end, and six members of the Friends gathered around. I nervously awaited a response while the photos were passed around the table. The response took a long time to come, finally from just one person—Mrs. Miller. Her enthusiasm was exciting and for me inspiring. I instantly realized a warm appreciation and affection for Flora Miller that was to continue for the rest of our relationship—till the end of her life. As the meeting broke up, the last as well as the first word was from Flora Miller: "Don't let that Calder get away from us."

As time went on I got to know Flora's unfailing warmth and enthusiasm for the new people and new art that she was attracting to the Whitney. The years during which she headed the Board paved the way for all the future successes of the Whitney Museum.

Howard Lipman is a founding partner of the invest-ment firm of Neuberger & Berman, with which he has been associated for more than forty-five years. He has been a Trustee of the Whitney Museum of American Art since 1969, and served as President of the Museum (1974–77), Chairman of the Board (1977–85), and Chairman of the Search Committee that found the Museum's current Director, Tom Armstrong. Howard Lipman and his wife, Jean, have given more works of art to the Whitney Museum than any other patrons except Gertrude Vanderbilt Whitney.

Left: Alexander Calder, *The Cock's Comb*, 1960, painted sheet iron, collection of the Whitney Museum of American Art. This work was purchased in 1962 by the Friends of the Whitney Museum of American Art as the result of the overwhelming enthusiasm for it by Flora and Howard Lipman. At the time, Howard Lipman was Chairman of the Acquisitions Committee of the Friends, which included Arthur G. Altschul, Mrs. Ira Haupt, Mrs. Frederick W. Hilles, and Charles Simon.

Gertrude Vanderbilt Whitney was a professional sculptor who received many public commissions for the design of monuments throughout the world, a number of which are still extant. Flora surrounded herself with her mother's sculpture, as well as contemporary works. The traditional association of sculpture and the Whitney Museum of American Art, maintained and encouraged by Flora, is illustrated in the following photographs:

Top right: Installation view of *Summer Exhibition of the Permanent Collection*, 1932, at the Whitney Museum of American Art, 10 West Eighth Street.

Center right: Installation view of *Contemporary American Sculpture: Selection I*, April 5–May 15, 1966, at the Whitney Museum of American Art, 22 West Fifty-fourth Street. The sculptures illustrated were acquired by the Museum through the generosity of Howard and Jean Lipman who, more than any other patrons, have expanded the collection of sculpture in the Permanent Collection of the Whitney Museum.

Lower right: Installation view of the Permanent Collection, featuring sculpture, in the new Whitney Museum, 945 Madison Avenue, designed by Marcel Breuer, 1966.

Ezra Stoller © ESTO

Fulfillment of a Legacy

Eliza Parkinson Cobb
C. Douglas Dillon

Flora talking with Eliza Parkinson (Cobb), President of the Museum of Modern Art, and Lloyd Goodrich, Director of the Whitney Museum of American Art, October 20, 1964.

Flora Miller's mother, Gertrude Vanderbilt Whitney, founded the Whitney Museum, and Flora carried the torch for her and built it into the important institution it is today. My aunt, Lillie P. Bliss, was one of the three lady founders of the Museum of Modern Art, and she and Mrs. Whitney were friends. It so happened that during a brief part of the time that Flora was President of the Whitney Museum, I was President of the Modern. So far as we knew, during those years, we were the only women presidents of any museum. This gave us a very cozy feeling toward each other—a feeling of something shared—and we used to greet one another at exhibition openings and such occasions, with a little private laughter and much affection, as can be seen in this photo with Lloyd Goodrich.

I remember going to an exhibition with Flora of pictures by Demuth and others of that era. I will never forget the deep joy she seemed to experience. She was truly devoted and dedicated not only to the Museum as such, but to art itself.

She was also truly cosmopolitan and one of my most delightful memories is of calling on her, with René d'Harnoncourt, in her beautiful house in Paris. It had been her mother's house and studio, and Flora and her husband, Macculloch Miller, spent time there every year. They were very much at home in the life of Paris.

Eliza Parkinson Cobb

Flora with C. Douglas Dillon, President of the Metropolitan Museum of Art, as he received the 1975 Skowhegan Gertrude Vanderbilt Whitney Award for outstanding patronage and support of the arts at the Skowhegan School Awards dinner.

This picture illustrates one of the most memorable evenings of my life. It was special to me because on that evening, Flora Miller made the effort to attend the Annual Skowhegan School Awards dinner and personally present me with the Gertrude Vanderbilt Whitney award.

I looked upon Flora Miller as a legendary figure who exemplified all that was best in the art and museum worlds of New York. Her graciousness in taking the trouble to present the award touched me very much.

We had become friends over the years in Jupiter Island, where we both spent time in the winter, but after this particular evening we became much closer and often discussed the common problems and challenges facing the Metropolitan and the Whitney museums.

Indeed, when her daughter, Flora Biddle, was to take her turn at accepting responsibility for managing the Whitney, she introduced us, and we three talked together about our common interests in the two institutions. I like to think that these conversations played a role in cementing the close and friendly relations that exist between the Metropolitan and the Whitney.

As one privileged to enjoy the friendship of Flora Miller, I benefited from the warmth, kindness and sweetness that always characterized her nature. She had a totally remarkable combination of strength and clarity of vision with undisputed feminine charm.

It is with great pleasure that I add my tribute to the many honoring the memory of this great lady.

C. Douglas Dillon

Eliza Parkinson Cobb has been a Trustee of the Museum of Modern Art since 1939, served as President (1965–68), and is currently Vice Chairman.

C. Douglas Dillon, Ambassador to France (1953–57) and Secretary of the Treasury (1961–65), among other government appointments, was a Trustee of the Metropolitan Museum of Art (1951–53, 1965–85), and served as President (1970–78) and Chairman of the Board (1978–83).

The following remarks were delivered by Flora at a party on May 18, 1977 in celebration of her daughter, Flora, becoming President of the Whitney Museum of American Art. The occasion also honored two other Presidents, David M. Solinger and Howard Lipman:

"My mother had a small dinner party, mostly of artists, on the opening of the Whitney Museum on Eighth Street and she made a little speech, which was rare for her to do. It truly was an exciting event and the small museum was a cozy and lovely place. All the openings were fun—and I mean truly great fun—artists whose works were on exhibition and friends of theirs would be drinking happily and looking at their own pictures or sculptures. When we moved to Fifty-fourth Street I was so concerned that the openings would not have that joyful and intimate air that my mother had created, but I think they had, if to a slightly lesser degree. Mrs. Force did much to create that "fun" on Eighth Street—and she was a great protector and friend of my mother.

My mother left the Museum to me when she died. She said I could sell it or keep it. Imagine if I had sold the greatest museum of American art in the world! My contribution during all the years I was President was to move the Museum to this inspired building that Marcel Breuer and Hamilton Smith designed, and that was constructed by them with the help of Michael Irving, my architect son-in-law, who had much to do with the planning. Now my daughter, Flora, as the President, is doing a truly marvelous job, and no one would have been more proud of her than her grandmother, Gertrude Vanderbilt Whitney."

Robert Henri, *Gertrude Vanderbilt Whitney*, 1916, oil on canvas, collection of the Whitney Museum of American Art, Gift of Flora Whitney Miller. Flora cherished this painting of her mother and made it a gift to the Whitney Museum to ensure that this dramatic image of the founder of the Museum would always be presented to the public.

The Gift of History

S. Dillon Ripley
Frederick A. Cushing

It was a joy on June 5, 1981 to be reunited with members of the Gertrude Vanderbilt Whitney family at a ceremony in connection with a gift to the Archives of American Art from Mrs. Whitney's granddaughter, Flora Miller Biddle, of the papers of the celebrated founder of the Whitney Museum. The luncheon was in honor of Mrs. Whitney's daughter Flora Miller, and was made delightful by her sparkling presence. Mrs. Miller inherited all of the charm of her mother, Gertrude Vanderbilt Whitney, and the passionate dedication to the lives of the artists and collectors who illuminated her mother's life. I myself was fascinated by Mrs. Whitney, who in 1930 courageously founded what has now become the international repository of American art, the Whitney Museum in New York. In the early days there was a considerable struggle for recognition, but I can remember always the commanding figure of Mrs. Whitney, who occupied such a signal position in New York in the world of culture at the time. It was the beginning of museums of modern art and the Whitney took its place along with the Museum of Modern Art in strengthening the understanding of American art in this country. The almost simultaneous founding of these two museums was a recognition and a fulfillment of the tradition established by the Armory Show of 1913—that New York had come of age and that American art was here to stay. This was an exciting period, coincident with the Great Depression but stimulated by the sagacity of such figures as Mrs. Whitney and the dealers who were just beginning to be well recognized, from the Voses in Boston to Edith Halpert and Marian Willard in New York.

Some of the electricity of the period was evoked by Mrs. Miller at our luncheon in 1981. Reminiscences streamed in from all assembled. With Tom Armstrong and John Baur, two of the Directors of the Whitney Museum, we lacked only Lloyd Goodrich to reinforce some of the feelings of the beginnings. Mrs. Miller and I chatted extensively about the Whitney studio in Long Island and only wished that the celebration could have been held there, as it would evoke even more memories of the time.

Gertrude Vanderbilt Whitney involved herself in an extraordinary variety of activities. These are beautifully demonstrated in the archives of letters and materials given to the Smithsonian. In addition to novelettes, plays, writings of an enormous variety, there is the wealth of correspondence, both artistic and social, including fascinating accounts of who came to dinner and when and how they were placed around the table! This detail encompasses a whole panorama of American life in and around New York, Newport, Paris, and during World War I, evocative and reminiscent of Mrs. Whitney's vibrant and characteristically energetic charms. Mrs. Whitney personified these times in her responses to life on the broadest scale, from art to landscape, from society to the realities of the hospital and war. Mrs. Whitney, known as a distinguished sculptor, was of course a diarist and confidante of almost all the American artists of the period. This trove of material someday will help to set the cap on the history of New York in the first four decades of this century. It is an enormous pleasure for the Smithsonian to be associated with the history of American art in this vibrant manner.

S. Dillon Ripley

Flora with her family at a reception celebrating the gift of Gertrude Vanderbilt Whitney's papers to the Archives of American Art, Smithsonian Institution, June 5, 1981. Seated are: Flora and Cornelius Vanderbilt (Sonny) Whitney; standing are (from left): Flora Biddle, Leverett S. Miller and his wife, Linda Miller.

Flora at the publication party for *Gertrude Vanderbilt Whitney*, a biography by B.H. Friedman with the research collaboration of Flora Miller Biddle, September 21, 1978, surrounded by her great-grandson, Anthony Evans (second from right), and descendants of artists she had known as a child (from left): Jacques Davidson (son of Jo Davidson), Howard Cushing and Fred Cushing (grandsons of Howard Cushing).

The occasion of the publication of *Gertrude Vanderbilt Whitney* by B.H. Friedman in collaboration with Mrs. Whitney's granddaughter Flora was the first time I met Mrs. Miller. I had long admired the portrait my grandfather [Howard Cushing] had painted of her as a child and found that the special qualities he captured in this portrait of a little girl had certainly materialized in her mature life. Howard Cushing and Gertrude Whitney had a very close and supportive friendship which continued throughout his short, but prolific life. They seemed to share that special bond which exists between artists. In his studio in Newport, there are two of Mrs. Whitney's bronzes which were gifts to my grandfather, and he did his early explorations as a muralist at her studio in Old Westbury,

as well as producing two portraits of her daughter and one of her, which is now in the collection of the Whitney Museum.

I met Mrs. Miller on several occasions after this pleasant evening, and was delighted with her stories and reminiscences of her childhood and of my grandfather. One always wishes for more time with such a wonderful person, but I feel very privileged to have known Flora Miller and to have touched the past through her amusing and always kind anecdotes of a more gentle time.

Frederick A. Cushing

S. Dillon Ripley, distinguished zoologist and museum director, served as Secretary of the Smithsonian Institution (1964–84) and is currently Secretary Emeritus.

Frederick A. Cushing is an independent video producer whose firm, Telltale Associates, produces documentary films. He is the grandson of Howard Cushing, who was a close friend of Gertrude Vanderbilt Whitney and who painted the portrait of Flora which appears as the frontispiece to this book.

Flora, The Divine One

Diana Vreeland
Bronson Winthrop Chanler

Flora, the Divine One.

Flora—beautiful, bewildering, and magnetic with an enchanting laugh. Her voice, her appearance, and her thoroughness in every form of charm was wonderful.

Flora was flirtatious and gave away charm beguilingly. She was naughty, very naughty. She loved fun and laughter as children do.

Flora was a very private person, almost mysterious. She was an elusive beauty and was not seen everywhere. Flora was unique, remarkable, and will never be replaced.

We will always miss her.

Diana Vreeland

Above, right: Flora, c. 1900.

Left: Flora and a young friend in their bathing costumes at Seabright, New Jersey, 1914.

Top, left: Flora in the Adirondacks, c. 1913.

Facing page: Flora photographed by Cecil Beaton, c. 1932.

Below: Flora and her mother, Gertrude Vanderbilt Whitney, in the paddock at Belmont Park, c. 1930.

Facing page: Album page with photographs of Flora in traditional attire for riding sidesaddle in the celebration at Aiken of the 50th anniversary of the founding of polo, 1932 (top); and Flora at Camp "Bliss" in the Adirondacks, 1936. Flora and Cully built this camp for themselves on Little Tupper Lake in the Adirondacks and spent many happy summer days there trout fishing in Charlie Pond Stream.

F.W.M. - "BLISS" - 1936

Somehow it seems to me that Flora managed to keep about her in the 1980s the aura of the style and the gaiety of the 1920s. It was somehow contagious, and being around her made one want to be as charming and as gay and as witty as one could.

Bronson Winthrop Chanler

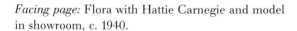

Facing page: Flora with Hattie Carnegie and model in showroom, c. 1940.

Above, left: Flora and Cully in the garden of Winfield House, the residence of the American Ambassador to the Court of St. James, preparing to attend a party given by Flora's cousin, John Hay (Jock) Whitney, American Ambassador (1956–61).

Above, right: Flora entering the exhibition *American Women of Style* at the Metropolitan Museum of Art with her granddaughter Fiona Irving (left) and her daughter Flora Biddle, December 10, 1975. The exhibition, organized by Diana Vreeland, Special Consultant, Costume Institute, featured Gertrude Vanderbilt Whitney.

Diana (Mrs. T. Reed) Vreeland is Special Consultant, Costume Institute, Metropolitan Museum of Art, and was fashion editor of Harper's Bazaar *(1937–62) and editor of* Vogue *(1962–71).*

Bronson Winthrop "Bim" Chanler is the son of Flora's childhood friend, Leslie Murray, and her husband, Louis Stuyvesant Chanler. His great-uncle was Robert Winthrop Chanler, the eccentric artist and friend of Gertrude Vanderbilt Whitney. Robert Winthrop Chanler, known as "Sheriff Bob" after he successfully ran for the office of sheriff of Dutchess County, New York, painted the murals in Gertrude Vanderbilt Whitney's bedroom in the Old Westbury studio, as well as those in her MacDougal Alley studio.

Family Places

Gertrude Conner
Linda Shearer
Tom Armstrong

I've always remembered what Flora said to me back in 1940, in her living room in Old Westbury. "Roots are so important. Someday you'll have a family and a home. Hold on to your established home. It brings strength." And she retained her family place to the end of her life.

Gertrude Conner

Top left: The rose garden at Old Westbury, spring, c. 1931.

Lower left: Dining room of Flora's home in Old Westbury, 1986.

Top right and facing page: Flora's residence on the Whitney property in Old Westbury, the beloved home with which her family and friends always identified her. The house was designed by Stewart, Walker and Gillette in 1924 and built in 1925.

Top of page: The "French House" in Old Westbury, designed by William Adams Delano, c. 1925–27. When her children were very young, Flora moved to this house, known as the "French House" because of its Norman style, which had been built for her on the Whitney family property by her father, Harry Payne Whitney. He had originally planned it for Flora and her first husband, Roderick Tower, but they divorced before it was completed.

Above: Château du Boulay, "Le Petit Boulay," near Tours in the Loire Valley. Every year or so during the late 1920s and early 1930s, Flora and her family would spend a few weeks at Le Boulay, which had belonged to her mother, Gertrude Vanderbilt Whitney. It was ruined during World War II by the German forces who used it as a military headquarters.

Facing page: Album page with photographs of "Le Petit Boulay," 1929.

Flora Whitney Miller had a grandeur and a style that was unique; she had authority, but was sympathetic and understanding, and most of all, she had a twinkle in her eye—all of which, I realize now, had a tremendous impact on me as a child.

In thinking how I became interested in art, it somehow goes back to Mrs. Miller. Without a doubt, one of the highlights of my life was staying all alone with Mr. and Mrs. Miller in their Paris apartment when I was a teenager; they truly made me feel like a princess!

Linda Shearer

Top left: Façade of Gertrude Vanderbilt Whitney's studio on the rue Boileau in Paris, c. 1914. From the time she was a young child, Flora visited her mother's studio in Paris. After she inherited it, she continued to enjoy the Paris studio with Cully, members of her family and many friends who visited her at this residence, until she sold it in 1972.

Lower left: Courtyard of Gertrude Vanderbilt Whitney's studio on the rue Boileau in Paris, c. 1914.

Facing page: Living room of Flora's home at 10 Gracie Square, 1986. For many years, *Juliet and Her Nurse* by J.M.W. Turner hung over the Venetian Baroque piano.

Throughout her life, Flora carried with her
many decorative objects representing her
heritage from the splendor of Whitney and
Vanderbilt residences. She possessed a style
for combining and arranging objects she
acquired to make her homes distinctively
fanciful and welcoming places. Her strong
attraction to the unusual made visiting her
like going to the magic kingdom of a real
spellbinder. Her response to color and
design expressed her enchantment with
the romantic aspects of life as well as her
vitality and strength.

Tom Armstrong

Below: Interior of 871 Fifth Avenue, childhood home of Flora, designed by Stanford White. Flora kept the marble arched frame surrounding the door in the center of the photograph when the house was destroyed in 1942, and installed it later in her apartment at 10 Gracie Square.

Bottom of page: Second floor hall of Flora's duplex apartment at 10 Gracie Square, one of her homes from about 1948 until her death, with marble arched door frame from 871 Fifth Avenue surrounding the doorway to the upstairs sitting room. The sculpture on the pedestal is *Daphne*, a 1933 bronze by her mother, Gertrude Vanderbilt Whitney.

Facing page: Foyer of Flora's residence at 544 East Eighty-sixth Street, a building owned by Cully which was one of their homes from about 1928 to 1948, with embossed doors she subsequently moved to her apartment at 10 Gracie Square.

Gertrude Conner; biographical note, p. 27.

Linda Shearer, the youngest child of Frances Goodwin and Ivor G. Balding, was affiliated with the Solomon R. Guggenheim Museum (1969–80) and was Associate Curator there when she left to become Director of Artists Space (1980–85), a not-for-profit gallery in New York City. She is now Curator in the Department of Painting and Sculpture at the Museum of Modern Art.

Tom Armstrong; biographical note, p. 126.

Grande Doyenne

Gloria Vanderbilt
Gertrude Conner

Flora with her cousin Gloria Vanderbilt and her daughter Flora, Skowhegan Awards Dinner, 1978.

How lovely her spirit was! And never more apparent than on Thanksgiving when annually family and friends would meet, traveling from near and far, to celebrate the day at the LeBoutillier's. How eagerly awaited her arrival, timed always after all had gathered . . . the flurry of anticipation as the great door opened and there she would be with a vivid and shimmering quality; white and red and black meticulously jumbling together from the colored silks she wore, the translucent skin, the luscious Chinese lacquer of her nails, the marigold of jewels, earrings of pearl close to hair coiffed tenderly as the feathers of a bird. She was indeed resplendent to welcome as she made her way to the sofa placed by the fireside in the room that had once been her mother's studio. There she would sit, ensconced in her usual place, with an air of serenity that was at the same time receptive and inviting; there was gaiety too, as if she expected that lovely things were about to happen, which drew us, each in turn, to sit by her side, catch up on family gossip and pay homage. Although the times my cousin Flora and I saw each other were far too few—just to know that she was *there* mattered to me, a lot. It gave me a sense of family and belonging and, now, although I will not see her again, it is in this way that she resides in the geography of my mind: steadfast. Memory is like that. Even when I'm not thinking of her, she's there. Then there are other moments, unexpected, when an image of her comes to me . . . the gesture of her hand as it reached out to me that last time I saw her, and a poem from long ago circles around in my head. "I know a lady sweet and kind, was never face so pleased my mind, I did but see her passing by and yet I love her til I die." I hope she knew.

Gloria Vanderbilt

Flora surrounded by members of her family at the Skowhegan Awards Dinner, 1975. From left: Pamela T. LeBoutillier; Gertrude Conner and her husband, McCauley Conner, and daughter Barbara Gabaldoni; Flora's cousin John Payson; her grandson Whitney Tower, Jr. (seated); Flora; Nancy Payson, John Payson's wife at the time; Sandra Payson; Flora Biddle and her husband at the time, Michael H. Irving.

When the Skowhegan Awards Dinners were begun in 1971, the Gertrude Vanderbilt Whitney Patron of the Arts Award was established to honor outstanding patrons of the arts. As often as possible, Flora attended with members of the family, making this Award meaningful and distinguished by her presence. She was the grande doyenne of a family of beaming, proud admirers. The initiation of the Award was recently described to Flora's daughter, Flora Miller Biddle, by John Eastman, Jr., Trustee of the Skowhegan School of Painting and Sculpture, in a letter dated January 23, 1987:

"I dreamt one night that in as much as Skowhegan's basic program is to help young artists and [Gertrude Vanderbilt Whitney] did so much in supporting and encouraging young artists, why not honor all she did for American art by likening the names and calling our Patron award "The Skowhegan Gertrude Vanderbilt Whitney Award."

I called Gerta [Flora's niece, Gertrude Conner] and found she liked the idea. Thus, I asked if she would check with her mother [Barbara Headley], her aunt Flora, and her uncle Cornelius Vanderbilt Whitney. She got back to me later to say they were enthusiastic.

I then telephoned Lloyd Goodrich for the Museum's reaction. He was equally enthusiastic. Thus the Skowhegan Gertrude Vanderbilt Whitney Award was started at our first Dinner in 1971.

I also felt it would be meaningful to the recipients if the Award was presented by relatives of Gertrude Vanderbilt Whitney."

This photo was taken of Auntie Flora at the Skowhegan School of Painting's Awards Dinner. She had very kindly agreed to present the Gertrude Vanderbilt Whitney Patron of the Arts Award.

Her jewels were always carefully chosen to complement her beautiful clothes. As is evident here, she was always perfectly dressed.

No matter what the circumstances, whether in the Adirondacks, the ground-breaking ceremonies of the Whitney Museum, or the most formal gala, she was regal and graceful.

As an expression of wonder, she would purse her lips and exclaim, "I *don't* believe it."

Gertrude Conner

Gloria Vanderbilt, artist, actress, author, and fashion designer, is Flora's first cousin. She is the daughter of Gertrude Vanderbilt Whitney's brother, Reginald Claypoole Vanderbilt, and Gloria Morgan Vanderbilt. She spent much of her youth in the care of Gertrude Vanderbilt Whitney.

Gertrude Conner; biographical note, p. 27.

Flora with her niece Gertrude Conner (right) and her daughter Flora, Skowhegan Awards Dinner, 1979.

On the Block

Benno C. Schmidt
John L. Marion

On two separate, extraordinary occasions, Flora secured the future of the Whitney Museum of American Art by selling objects very important to her and to the history of her family. First, when funds were being raised for the building of the Whitney Museum on Madison Avenue at Seventy-fifth Street, she gave Jeune Fille Qui Marche dans l'Eau *by Aristide Maillol and* The Smoker (Le Fumeur) *by Edouard Manet, both of which she had inherited from her mother, Gertrude Vanderbilt Whitney, to be auctioned for the benefit of the Whitney Museum's building and endowment campaign. And to initiate the effort to expand the present Whitney Museum, she sold* Juliet and Her Nurse *by J.M.W. Turner, making the first, and most significant, gift from a portion of the proceeds, which launched this campaign for the future.*

Facing page: Flora talking with John L. Marion while awaiting the auction of her painting by J.M.W. Turner, *Juliet and Her Nurse*, conducted at Sotheby's at 10:15 a.m. on May 29, 1980. Flora is sitting with her children, Flora Biddle and Whitney Tower.

Flora Whitney Miller was a remarkable lady. When I joined the Whitney Museum Board in 1964, primarily to help with fund-raising for the Marcel Breuer building at Seventy-fifth and Madison Avenue, I soon learned that Flora was the heart and soul of the Whitney Museum. What she lacked in physical strength was more than made up in commitment, dedication, wisdom and love, and her leadership as President of the Museum was the inspiration that enabled us to move closer to her dream.

Benno C. Schmidt

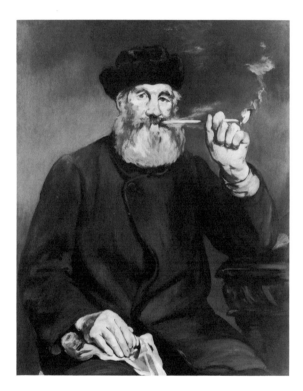

Left: Aristide Maillol, *Jeune Fille Qui Marche dans l'Eau (Étude pour l'Île de France)*, c. 1910, bronze. Gertrude Vanderbilt Whitney originally owned this sculpture, which Flora donated to the auction at Parke-Bernet on May 11, 1966 for the benefit of the building and endowment fund for the new Whitney Museum of American Art on Madison Avenue at Seventy-fifth Street.

Above: Edouard Manet, *The Smoker (Le Fumeur)*, 1866, oil on canvas, collection of the Minneapolis Institute of Arts, Gift of Mr. and Mrs. Bruce B. Dayton. Flora inherited this work from her mother, Gertrude Vanderbilt Whitney. Before the May 11, 1966 benefit auction, Flora sold her Manet in a regular sale at Parke-Bernet on October 14, 1965, and donated the proceeds to the building and endowment fund for the new Museum.

I first met Mrs. Miller in the mid-1960s when she came to Sotheby's as a client. She was a grand lady, and was, of course, in the beginning, a symbol to me of the Whitney Museum —as she was to so many others. Later, I came to know her better and it was always a pleasure to talk with her about her many interests and her loves. One of the highlights of my career occurred on May 29, 1980, when I was privileged to share with Mrs. Miller one moment that combined two of her greatest passions—the Whitney Museum and her Turner.

Juliet and Her Nurse by J.M.W. Turner was a part of Mrs. Miller's personal history as it was the favorite painting in her private collection. When she changed residences from her New York apartment to her country home in the summer, the painting would always accompany her there. Originally, the picture had been brought to America at the turn of the century by her great-uncle, Colonel O.H. Payne, and it was then considered the most celebrated painting by Turner to remain in private hands. It has been described by Martin Butlin, Keeper of the Historic British Collection at the Tate Gallery, as "perhaps the most splendid of all Turner's paintings of the 1830s." *Juliet and Her Nurse*, exhibited at the Royal Academy in 1836, depicts Shakespeare's Juliet with her nurse beside her watching from their balcony as a festive crowd gathers during a dazzling and enchanted evening in the Piazza San Marco in Venice.

In a gesture that would part her from the painting she loved, but would also benefit the Museum she loved, Mrs. Miller consigned the Turner to Sotheby's for auction. She knew it would be widely sought after, as did I. Neither of us, however, could anticipate that it would make auction history.

On the day the Turner was to be sold, Mrs. Miller arrived at the gallery surrounded by her family and friends. The salesroom was filled to capacity with international art press and an excited audience of art lovers and connoisseurs eager to witness this special event. As I made my way to the auctioneer's rostrum, I stopped to greet Mrs. Miller, who was seated in the first row of the salesroom. When I leaned forward to wish her good luck she whispered in response to me, "You'll do just fine." Inspired by that gracious reassurance, I took my position. A hush fell over the room as I began the auction. Rather quickly the bidding passed the $2.5 million mark. The silence in the auction room was punctuated only by the sound from the two bidders—one over the telephone calling from London, the other present in the salesroom. In 6 minutes 4 seconds, I brought the hammer down for a record $6.4 million ($7.04 million with premium), the highest price at that time ever paid at auction for any work of art. As the salesroom audience broke into applause I looked over to the first row and watched as Mrs. Miller, her family and friends beside her, congratulated each other and made their way out for a true celebration.

While I have been privileged over the past twenty-five years to have experienced a few such special moments at the rostrum, those moments are rare and highly prized. I will not forget this moment of history. Nor will I forget the special style and grace of the woman who had made it possible.

John L. Marion

J.M.W. Turner, *Juliet and Her Nurse*, 1836, oil on canvas. When Flora's painting was sold by Sotheby's on May 29, 1980, it brought the highest price at that time ever paid at auction for any work of art.

Looking Ahead

Fiona Irving

Three generations of Whitneys—Flora, her daughter Flora Biddle, and her granddaughter Fiona Irving, October 1979. In 1970, Flora Biddle decided to return to school to obtain an undergraduate degree. Her thesis topic was her grandmother, Gertrude Vanderbilt Whitney. In the course of her research, she came upon a vast quantity of previously undiscovered material that became the basic resource for the biography *Gertrude Vanderbilt Whitney* by B.H. Friedman. Her daughter Fiona Irving is now completing her Ph.D. in Art History at Columbia University. The legacy of service to American art thus continues from Flora to her daughter to her granddaughter.

When I look at this photograph, I imagine my grandmother, having noticed the photographer, warmly cooing in her inimitable fashion, "Ooooh." Among other attributes, this sound, like my grandmother, was full of elegance, wonder and curiosity, as well as humor and empathy. She said it while watching TV (which she loved), observing the Mets (whose games she never missed), hearing intriguing news of her family and acquaintances, and even eating ice cream. She was a cheerful confidante to her grandchildren—interested in hearing about all aspects of our lives and thoughtfully giving advice, while sharing with us colorful stories about herself. She had an eye for charming people and beautiful objects, especially painting and sculpture. She was of course particularly interested in the Whitney Museum. When I visited her she seemed fascinated to hear about the variety of exhibitions and events taking place there. Through amusing anecdotes about her mother's place in the art world, as well as her own, she instilled in me a sense of pride at having the opportunity to be involved in the Museum founded by my great-grandmother. And in doing so, she reminded me that as she had taken responsibility for ensuring that her mother's goals for the Whitney Museum endured, so should I and the rest of our family. Her joy in having supported the Museum was infectious. Of special concern to her, I gathered, was maintaining what she saw as the Museum's unique commitment to American artists—not just by exhibiting an artist's work, but by providing support on a more personal level, as her mother had done. She had a wonderful way of encouraging me by her example, as an older friend would do.

Fiona Irving, art historian, is one of four children of Flora Biddle and Michael H. Irving. She currently lives with her husband, Peter Wold, in Minneapolis, where she is Curator of American Art at the University Art Museum, University of Minnesota.

Epilogue

Tom Armstrong

To those who knew her in the last decade of her life, Flora Whitney Miller might have seemed removed from the daily events of the Whitney Museum of American Art. But in my sense of the history of the Museum, she always will be the most vital and essential part of the evolution of the institution. A number of visits to her home in Old Westbury, where we talked as she sat in her chair before a card table filled with correspondence and mementos, helped me realize that it was Flora, more than any other person, who was determined that the Whitney Museum should survive and surpass even the aspirations her mother had for it.

After Flora's death on July 18, 1986, I reviewed many of her papers. They revealed countless attempts to secure support from acquaintances, close friends, and family members in order to make the Whitney Museum a great institution devoted to quality in American art and sustained by public support. As I sat with her, next to the sun porch filled with sculpture from her mother's era, it was impossible not to recognize that even though Gertrude Vanderbilt Whitney will always be revered as the founder of the Whitney Museum, it was Flora who accomplished a more difficult task—to bring it from the domain of private wealth and personal concern for artists into the ranks of major public institutions, enjoyed and acclaimed by international audiences.

The view of where she once sat and faced me with cheer and resolute charm reminds me of the purpose and strength she established for our institution, a legacy which others are now dedicated to preserving and celebrating as the foundation for the future.

Tom Armstrong has been Director of the Whitney Museum of American Art since 1974.

Flora's living room in her Old Westbury home with her Chippendale chair before a card table—her worktable—close to the television. Silhouetted in the window is the sculpture *Jo Davidson* and, in the corner, *La Chinoise*, both by her mother. Watercolors on the bookcase are by her husband, Cully. On the sofa are her Mets baseball cap and needlework pillows, including one advising "Never Complain, Never Explain."

Photograph Credits

Many of the photographs in this publication are from family photograph albums and collections, courtesy of Flora Whitney Miller's children: Flora Miller Biddle, Pamela T. LeBoutillier, Leverett S. Miller, and Whitney Tower. The following list applies to photographs for which an additional acknowledgment is due.

Avery Architectural and Fine Arts Library, Columbia University: pp. 31 (lower left and right), 114 (top). Cecil Beaton: p. 103. Beidler-Viken: pp. 33, 109. Byron Collection, Museum of the City of New York: pp. 29, 30. Churchill Downs: p. 45. © Geoffrey Clements: pp. 2, 14 (left), 21, 24, 40 (upper and lower right), 53, 60, 66, 68 (bottom), 82 (left), 94, 95 (center), 98, 107, 108 (lower left), 121 (left), 127. Jerry Cooke/Pix, courtesy *Life Magazine*, copyright © Time Incorporated: p. 106. Bill Cunningham: pp. 116, 119. Almé Dupont, courtesy *Vogue*, copyright © 1916 (renewed 1944, 1946) by The Condé Nast Publications Inc.: p. 17 (top left). Brooks Edler: pp. 77, 81, 92 (top). Charlotte Fairchild: p. 19 (top). Freudy Photos, Inc.: pp. 54, 63, 64, 67. Lawrence Fried, courtesy *Vogue*, copyright © 1966 by The Condé Nast Publications Inc.: p. 75. Floride Green: p. 102 (right). Victor Greene Studio: p. 23 (lower right). © Harris & Ewing, Washington, D.C.: pp. 18, 51. John T. Hopf, courtesy The Preservation Society of Newport County: p. 37. Paul Hosefros, courtesy *The New York Times*, copyright © 1980 by The New York Times Company: p. 120. International News Photos, Inc.: p. 104. Peter A. Juley & Son, p. 39. George Platt Lynes: p. 95 (top). Raymond Medio: p. 90. © Helaine Messer: pp. 22, 91 (lower right), 99, 124. The Metropolitan Museum of Art: pp. 28, 44. Baron de Meyer: p. 40 (upper left). The Minneapolis Institute of Arts: p. 121 (right). Bert and Richard Morgan Studio: p. 46 (upper left). The New York Times Company, copyright © 1909, 1964, 1964 reprinted by permission: pp. 42, 78, 84. Tony Palmieri, courtesy *Women's Wear Daily*, copyright © 1978 by Fairchild Publications, Inc.—A Capital Cities/ABC Company: p. 100. Parke-Bernet Galleries Inc.: p. 31 (top). Pollitzer, Strong & Meyer: p. 27. The Queens Borough Public Library: pp. 68 (top), 72. Karen Radkai, courtesy *House & Garden*, copyright © 1984 by The Condé Nast Publications Inc: pp. 113, 114 (bottom). Percy Rainford: p. 43 (lower right). Stephanie Rancou: pp. 96 (bottom), 117. John D. Schiff: p. 17 (bottom right). Raphael Shammaa: pp. 85, 96 (top). Sotheby's: p. 123. William Taylor: p. 83 (right). Jerry L. Thompson: p. 83 (left). Anne Tishler: pp. 32, 111 (top). Underwood and Underwood, courtesy *Vogue*, copyright © 1918 (renewed 1944, 1946) by The Condé Nast Publications Inc.: p. 50 (lower left). John Waggaman: p. 40 (lower left). Wide World Photos, Inc.: p. 88. J. Edwin Williamsson: p. 52. *Women's Wear Daily*, copyright © 1966 by Fairchild Publications, Inc.—A Capital Cities/ABC Company: p. 86.

Flora Miller Biddle graciously assisted in all aspects of this project, particularly in collecting the reminiscences of her mother by family and friends.

Publication coordinated by
Tom Armstrong

Editorial Director
Joan Weakley

Editor
Sheila Schwartz

Researchers
Anita Duquette
Linda Gordon
Vicki Drake

Designer
Karen Salsgiver,
Homans/Salsgiver

Printer
Meriden-Stinehour Press

Typesetter
Trufont Typographers